Native American TRIBES

Robert Doster

Native American TRIBES

Norman Bancroft Hunt

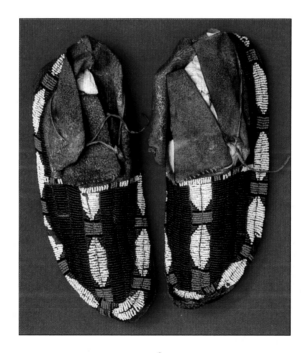

Regency House Publishing Ltd.

PAGE 2

*Navaho blankets and Apache 'conch' belt. The Southwest nurtured some
of the most spectacular and distinctive forms of creative expression on the
North American continent. Navaho blankets, with their bold colours and
designs, are unmistakable. The modern Apache belt, although using
commercially manufactured silver conch discs, is nevertheless an equally
distinctive form of Southwestern art.*

PAGE 3

*Plains beaded moccasins, probably Kiowan. The Indian aesthetic extended
to every aspect of their lives and great care was taken to ensure that even
simple everyday items of apparel, such as these moccasins, expressed their
sense of harmony with the world about them.*

RIGHT

*A Powhatan man. Among the first Native Americans to be encountered by
European colonists were the Powhatan of the Eastern Woodlands. Although
speaking dialects of the same Algonquian language, the Powhatan actually
consisted of a confederacy of approximately 200 villages from as many as
30 smaller tribes. The power and cohesion of the confederacy was held
together only by the charismatic leadership of Chief Powhatan, from
whom the confederacy derives its name.*

Published in 1997 by
Regency House Publishing Limited
3 Mill Lane
Broxbourne, Hertfordshire.
EN10 7AZ
United Kingdom

Copyright © 1997 Regency House Publishing Limited

ISBN 1 85361 4580

Printed in Italy

Contents

'The white men were frightened and called for soldiers. We had begged for life, and the white man thought we wanted their's. We heard that soldiers were coming. We did not fear. We hoped that we could tell them our troubles and get help.'

(Red Cloud, Sioux chief)

Introduction

The history of Indian-White relationships has been one of misunderstanding and distrust. The two ways of life were so dissimilar and so far apart that little common ground could be found between them, and this inevitably led to conflict. Neither side really understood the other. The history was, nevertheless, written by white chroniclers, because the Indians had no written language, and this was distorted the historical view since Indian opinion was rarely expressed.

We must, however, pause for a moment to consider what that Indian opinion may have been, and clues to this are contained in the translations of speeches and statements made by the spokesmen for the tribes. From such statements we can learn something of the complexity and diversity of the Indian life-style. Most people will already know something at least of the Plains warriors and hunters and their dependency on the buffalo and the acquisition of war honours, and will probably also have heard of the Apache tribes and the prolonged guerilla warfare they waged against the forces of the United States. Fewer, perhaps, will know of the mound cultures of the Southeast, the fishermen of the Northwest Coast, or the peace-loving Pueblo peoples of the Southwest.

The vastness of the area under consideration – which encompasses the whole of Canada and the United States, the Aleutian Islands, and part of northern Mexico – means that Native American people have had to cope with environmental conditions that ranged from arctic to sub-tropical, and their life-styles developed accordingly. Some were hunters, others were small farmers or large-scale agriculturalists, yet others had an almost exclusively seafaring economy.

It is difficult to place all these very different peoples into a common mould, yet there is nevertheless a certain feeling or sense in which they belong together and share a common background. Part of this, of course, is that they are the original inhabitants – the True Americans – whose history in the region goes back some 40,000 or more years. The white man's occupancy of only a few hundred years is paltry in comparison. But there is also another common, and deeper, factor that serves to unite the tribes: a deep love and respect for the land, and a sense of honour, chivalry, and respect for other people and for all living things. To the Indian, buffalo, bear, or deer is not merely an animal but is addressed as Brother.

This sense of equality extends to all aspects of the Indian world, since everything within it is considered animate and imbued with energy, motivation, and a spirit or 'soul'. Young Chief, a Cayuse leader, expressed this sense of 'belonging' in a treaty of 1855 that discussed the sale of Indian lands, which had been reserved 'for as long as the rivers shall run', so they could be opened for white settlement. In a short, but eloquent, speech he suggested the Treaty Commissioners should listen to the voices of the land: *'I wonder if the ground has anything to say? I wonder if the ground is listening to what is being said?'*

This book attempts to show something of the Indian view. Each chapter is organized so that the general environmental conditions and characteristic life-styles of a culture area are described, and this is followed by descriptions of the major tribal groups in each region. The speeches of chiefs, shamans (medicine men), and other prominent spokespeople are included as part of the text so that the authentic voice of the Native American is allowed to come through.

The Southwest

Although the topography of the Southwest varies considerably, from high mountains to deep canyons, the entire area is characterized as a region of semi-arid land located primarily in Arizona and New Mexico, but extending in the north into Utah and Colorado, south into the northern regions of Mexico, and west to the Nevada and southern California deserts.

It is an area of extremes: brilliant blue skies and intense summer heat and prolonged droughts may be followed by bitterly cold winters and deep snows. Short spring rains, often in the form of sudden downpours, result in extensive flash floods that bring life to dormant desert plants and create for a few, brief, days an abundance of colour and growth. For the rest of the year, passage through the region is hindered by cacti and the razor-sharp leaves of yucca and bear grass. The contrasts are summed up in this Pima Indian wind-song, sung shortly after the rains make their first appearance:

Far on the desert ridges

Stands the cactus;

Lo, the blossoms swaying

To and fro, the blossoms swaying, swaying.

The region is nevertheless classed as desert, and water is generally scarce. Annual precipitation is low and only the Rio Grande, the Colorado, San Juan and Gila Rivers and their tributaries, wind their way through here; but the tributaries are often dry and the major rivers inaccessible. When the Spanish expedition of 1540, led by Francisco Vásquez de Coronado, became the first Europeans to see the Grand Canyon which the Rio Grande had carved into the land, they bemoaned

the fact that their ablest climbers were unable to descend to the depths of the canyon, some $1\frac{1}{2}$ miles (2.4km) beneath the rim, to secure the precious water they required.

Yet, despite its unforgiving nature, the Southwest has nurtured some of the most impressive cultures to be found in North America. It has a long record of occupation by highly skilled agriculturalists, and Acoma Pueblo, or 'Sky City', located some 400 feet (120m) high on a mesa above the plain, has been occupied continuously for at least 1,000 years Acoma remains today much as it was when first founded.

The success and stability of Acoma and other Pueblo villages, as well as of the less formally organized but equally successful Pima and Papago, has been due to their ability to harness the forces the Southwest provides. Their ancestors, the Anasazi and Hohokam, had already tamed the desert by 600AD with a 250-mile-long network of irrigation canals, some of them 30 feet (9m) wide and 10 feet (3m) deep, and between them had brought nearly a quarter of a million square acres of land under cultivation.

Prior to that, the ancient cliff dwellers of Canyon de Chelly, Mesa Verde and other canyons of the Southwest, had established flourishing communities as early as the 4th century AD and built large multi-roomed apartment complexes from adobe (dried clay), with elaborate ritual complexes directed by Native American priests. Their modern descendants, the Pueblo tribes, occupy 19 pueblos, or towns, centred on the Rio Grande in New Mexico and speak either Keresan (Acoma, Cochiti, San Felipe, Santa Ana, Santo Domingo, Zia, Laguna) or Tanoan dialects (Taos, Isleta, Jemez, Picuris, San Juan, Sandia, Tesuque, Santa

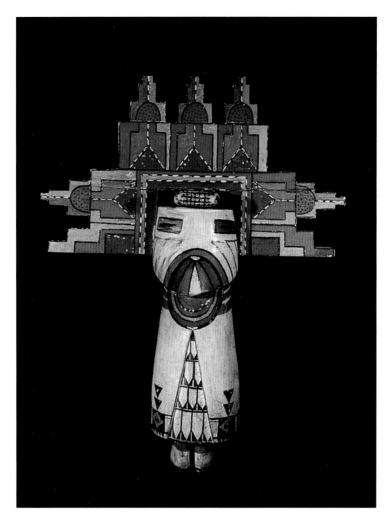

lara, San Ildefonso, Nambe), together with two isolated groups, the
uni and Hopi, who speak different languages.

Ranging around them, but relative newcomers to the area, are
numerous different Apache tribes and the related Navaho, who had a
well-developed hunting and trading culture. These people migrated south
from the subarctic regions of Canada and arrived in the Southwest only
shortly before the Spanish invasions, bringing with them a tradition of
hunting that differed dramatically from the slow seasonal cycles of
cultivation expressed by the Pueblo groups and by the Pima and Papago.
Unlike Pueblo belief, which sought to return everything to a centre of
balance and harmony, the Apache world was one of constant movement
and of immediate and spontaneous action.

Yet there was a sharing between these two very different traditions,
both in cultural influences and in trade, and at times the interaction was
so close that inter-marriages took place. There was conflict too, largely
instigated by the Apache groups who raided for anything they were
unable to secure by trade; yet at the same time there was a curious
balance between these desert dwellers that was of ultimate benefit to all.

This balance was disrupted in the 16th century with the arrival of the
Spanish, who attempted to impose their beliefs on the native peoples of
the Southwest, and continued under the domination of the area first by
Mexico, then independent Texas, and finally the United States, all of
whom waged wars of extermination against the various Apache groups
and attempted to subvert the influence of the Pueblo priests by
establishing churches within the precincts of the Pueblo towns.

The intrusions of these 'foreigners' were nevertheless largely
unsuccessful. The Pueblo groups continued to practise their ancient rites
in secret and to maintain their *kivas*, or underground ceremonial
chambers, whereas the Apache resisted attempts at domination and have
never been militarily defeated. Today the Pueblo tribes remain the most
conservative of North American Indian groups, retaining many of their
original beliefs and traditions and often refusing to become part of
mainstream American life. The Apache, by comparison, have adapted to
modern America, and, while continuing to observe earlier customs and
traditions and preserving their language, are dependent for tribal income
on leasing timber and mineral rights and providing hunting and fishing
licences and other access to recreational activities within their
reservation lands.

View in Pueblo Acoma N

The Pueblo Tribes

When the Spanish arrived in the Southwest in 1540 they listed 71 Pueblos in the area, many of which had been occupied for hundreds of years before the Spanish invasions.

Both Acoma and the Hopi village of Oraibi claim to be the oldest continuously occupied towns in the United States; although other Pueblos also show an ancient history. Cochiti and San Felipe were built about 1250AD as a result of a split of a larger Pueblo; and San Juan and Santa Clara were established in the 1300s.

Many of the ancient Pueblos disappeared under Spanish plans to consolidate the Southwest in a few, more manageable, areas, and the old village sites were abandoned. The population became concentrated in only a few locations, most of them established around 1700. Yet despite over 400 years of European influence, the Pueblo tribes continue to practise rituals and to hold to religious beliefs that are little changed since the 16th century.

For the Pueblo people life began in a series of underworlds, typically four, through which the people moved progressively upwards. Each of these worlds was a different colour – white, red, blue, and yellow – and according to the Indians of Santo Domingo the place of emergence into the present world was at Shipap, the Centre of the World. The Hopi Indians still make a shallow depression, or Sipapu, in the floors of their sacred *kivas* to mark this place where the people emerged and to which, at death, they must return.

Shipap was too imbued with power to be a place where the people could stay. Only Iatik, Mother of All, remained there; but before the people left she gave them her heart – which was made of corn – and told the priests about the ceremonies and rituals they were to conduct. The people then moved into the modern world, which had been made by Thought Woman who created all things by thinking them into existence.

Before the Creative Gods departed they gave the priests instructions in ways they could combine all the forces of the natural and supernatural worlds to maintain the precarious balance of an agricultural economy in a land of little rain, and the people were told that after death they would return to the innermost of the underworlds and be reborn as Shiwana, Rainmakers, who would return to the villages as clouds. The Shiwana live

> High up in the sky,
> See Rain-Makers seated,
> Hither come the rain-clouds now.
> Lovely! See the cloud, the cloud appear!
> Lovely! See the rain, the rain draw near!
> Who spoke?
> 'Twas the little corn-ear
> High on the tip of the stalk
> Saying while it looked at me
> Talking aloft there –
> 'Ah, perchance the floods
> Hither moving –
> Ah, may the floods come this way!'
> (Zuni Pueblo, songs sung while grinding corn)

Spanish thinking could not encompass the idea that the Pueblo tribes possessed an organized religion of their own. They considered the Pueblo Indians to be idolaters and attempted to impose the tenets of

ABOVE

The desert environment of the Southwest provided ample material for the manufacture of baskets, such as this Pima example. Both the Pima and Papago used linear patterns to depict the life-giving flow of water, although after 1900 these designs became more naturalistic in response to a demand for baskets for trade to Europeans.

OPPOSITE

Following Spanish incursions into the Southwest, many of the Pueblos relocated to the tops of mesas where they felt the difficulty of access afforded greater protection. Acoma Pueblo, also known as Sky City due to its magnificent location, was, however, founded in about 900AD, well before the arrival of the Spanish in the area, and claims with the Hopi village of Oraibi to be the oldest continually-occupied town in the United States.

The Southwest

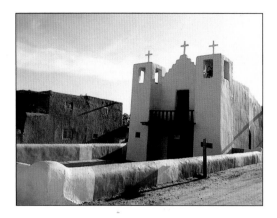

ABOVE
One of the most prominent features at virtually every Pueblo is the church, erected under the instigation of the Spanish using forced Indian labour. Despite nominal conversion to Catholicism, most Pueblo Indians see no contradiction in continuing to follow ancient rituals and ceremonies in addition to celebrating the Catholic mass.

OPPOSITE
Adobe dwellings, Acoma Pueblo.

Catholicism, to the extent that today most Pueblo Indians – with the exception of tribal groups at Hopi and Zuni – are at least nominal Catholics. In actuality, the forced religious beliefs of the Spanish had little real effect. Pueblo tradition is one of peaceful coexistence and of eclecticism, and few modern Pueblo inhabitants see any contradiction in celebrating mass in a Spanish-built church followed by Indian ceremonies in the church courtyard. To the Pueblo people, the adoption of Catholicism has been an enrichment of a traditional pattern of thinking rather than a denial of an ancient way of life.

The Spanish saw things differently. Their incursions into the Southwest were inspired by exaggerated tales of fabulous riches the region was reputed to hold; they had heard in Mexico that this was where the Seven Cities of Cibola, the Cities of Gold, were located, and it was in a search for these that they invaded the area; but this was combined with an evangelical zeal to convert the 'heathens'. Coronado's brutal suppression of the Pueblos in 1540 was followed by repeated Spanish demands for Pueblo submission and the eventual colonization of the area in 1598 by Don Juan de Onate.

Acoma resisted Onate's demands, and the Pueblo was stormed. Over 800 Indians were slaughtered, and all male prisoners over the age of 25 were ordered to have one foot amputated and to undergo 20 years of servitude in New Mexico; women over 25 merely had servitude imposed and were spared amputation. Two Hopis who happened to be visiting Acoma had their right hands cut off as a message to the other Pueblos of what they could expect should they offer any resistance to the Spanish.

Spanish depredations continued until, in 1680, Pueblo patience finally ran out. Under the leadership of Popé, a medicine man from San Juan who had been repeatedly beaten and whipped by the Spanish for refusing to abandon his old beliefs, all the Pueblo tribes, with the exception of Isleta and Piro, rose against the Spanish, killed most of the missionaries in the area together with several hundred other Spaniards, occupied Santa Fe, and drove the remaining Spanish back into Mexico.

Popé's fanatical hatred of the Spanish was crucial to the success of the Pueblo Revolt; yet this same hatred was ultimately to undermine the Pueblo groups and enable the Spanish to reinvade and reconquer the area between 1689 and 1692. Popé became more and more of a despot, meting out severe punishments – even execution – to anyone who

wavered at all from the traditional Indian ways. Even such a practical matter as using metal tools left behind by the Spanish could result in a brutal flogging from Popé and his followers. Thus, by the time the Spanish re-entered the area, Pueblo morale and solidarity had all but disappeared and they met with little organized resistance.

The only resistance to Spanish ideals stemmed from a passive refusal to abandon old ways of thinking or to wholeheartedly embrace the new ideas the Spanish sought to introduce. The priests continued to conduct the ancient ceremonies in secret and the introduction of the office of governor by the Spanish merely meant a change of name from the former government by a *cacique*, or priest-chief, rather than any real alteration in the way the Pueblos were organized.

Much of the ceremonialism, even during the period of Spanish domination, was intended to propitiate the powers that grant rain so that corn, the staple food product but also charged with intense ritual significance, would grow abundantly. The importance of rain is indicated in a song of the Tanoan-speaking Tewa Pueblos (Santa Clara, San Ildefonso, Nambe, Tesuque, and San Juan) who liken the sky to a loom in which the colours of morning, evening, rain and lightning, are woven:

> *O our Mother the Earth, O our Father the Sky,*
> *Your children are we, and with tired backs*
> *We bring you the gifts that you love.*
> *Then weave for us a garment of brightness;*
> *May the warp be the white light of morning,*
> *May the weft be the red light of evening,*
> *May the fringes be the falling rain,*
> *May the border be the standing rainbow.*
> *Thus weave for us a garment of brightness*
> *That we may walk fittingly where birds sing,*
> *That we may walk fittingly where grass is green,*
> *O our Mother the Earth, O our Father the Sky!*

The importance of rain and of rain-bringing ceremonies is evident in modern Pueblo life, which is still dependent to a large extent on agricultural produce. Although many Pueblo Indians are engaged in paid work off the reservations or depend on the sale of tourist crafts, as much as one third of tribal income may derive directly from planted crops. At Hopi the rains are encouraged by the ritual Hevebe songs of little girls,

The Southwest

RIGHT

The Apache, relatively recent arrivals in the Southwest, brought from their original subarctic homeland a belief in the presence of powerful supernaturals with curative powers. Combined with Southwestern beliefs in the fertility power of the Pueblo Kachinas, this resulted in the creation of the Gans, or Mountain Spirits, whose most prominent appearance is at a girl's puberty rites when, for four days, she is considered to be endowed with the ability to heal by touching those who seek her assistance. Following these rites she is considered to be fertile and of marriageable age.

OPPOSITE

One of the most accomplished achievements of the Pueblo tribes was the production of pottery, which continues to be a major craft industry in the Southwest today and is made both for utilitarian use and for the tourist market. This pot, from Zuni Pueblo, is a fine example of the stylized geometric forms characteristic of this area.

ho dance outside the houses while the adults sprinkle them with water.
sudden downpours during spring, the children may rush into the plaza
d rejoice in the refreshing rain brought by the long-invoked clouds.
such times they sing:

> *Hevebeta, come, come,*
> *Pour, pour down,*
> *Pour, pour down,*
> *Pour down, pour down,*
> *Pour down, pour down.*
>
> *Hither, flying cloud,*
> *Hither, flying cloud,*
> *Hither, flying cloud,*
> *Sprinkle me,*
> *Sprinkle me,*
> *Cloud, come bathe me!*
> *Hither hasten,*
> *Hither hasten,*
> *Come, come, come, come.*
>
> *Pour, pour down,*
> *Pour, pour down,*
> *Oh, change me now,*
> *Oh, change me now*
> *Into a cluster of flowers,*
> *Into a cluster of showers!*
>
> *Hevebeta, come, come,*
> *Pour, pour down,*
> *Pour, pour down,*
> *Pour down, pour down,*
> *Pour down, pour down.*

Continual references to Rain, Corn, and to Earth Mother in Pueblo
ual indicate that agriculture is far more than just a practical art. A
odern Hopi, in fact, is said to spend half his life in activities of a
remonial nature, which include tending the corn-fields, since planting,
owth, and harvesting are all felt to be imbued with sacred meaning.

The importance of corn is further emphasized by the fact that the Corn
Dance, traditionally held during spring and summer, may be performed
at other times of the year to mark the inauguration of the Pueblo's
secular officers or on the occasion of the Pueblo's saint's day.

Perhaps the most spectacular Corn Dance is that of Santo Domingo,

The Southwest

Although it is impossible to identify this Kachina with any certainty, it is nevertheless a characteristic type of Hopi Kachina doll and displays a number of features that would be familiar to anyone watching Kachina dances. Note, in particular, the dance apron and sash, protruding eyes, and snout-like mouth. The Kachina carries a rattle in its right hand and would formerly have held something else, such as a sprig of evergreen to indicate longevity, in its left, though this has now been lost.

held on the 4th of August, Saint Dominic being the Pueblo's patron saint. Santo Domingo, like other Rio Grande Pueblos, is divided into two moieties or halves: the Squash, or Winter People, and the Turquoise or Summer People. Each is responsible for the management of Pueblo affairs for six months of the year. The dancers of each moiety perform alternately during the Corn Dance, the Koshares (or Delight-Makers) of the Turquoise People appearing before the Kurenas of the Squash People.

Both the Koshares and the Kurenas are believed to be the spirits of the deceased who possess power to bring rain clouds and, thereby, to encourage the growth of crops. They magically protect the Pueblo from harm, and, by performing as clowns, remind the people of their fallibility and of the fact that only the gods are perfect. The Koshares and Kurenas are similar in some respects to the Kachinas of other Pueblos, since the Kachinas are also the returned spirits of the deceased and are considered to be Rainmakers.

The Kachina cult itself is most prominent at the Hopi and Zuni villages, where masked dancers representing the Kachinas are present in the villages for six months of the year. The major ceremony at Zuni is that of the Shalako, during which the spirits of the dead return to be honoured and fed. The Shalako is a re-enactment of the Zuni emergence and migration myths, as well as being a prayer for rain and for the well-being of the people.

The principal performers at the Shalako are the Shalako themselves, considered to be messengers of the Rainmakers; Sayatasha, the Rain God of the North; Hututu, the Rain God of the South; Sholawitsi, the Fire God (representative of the Sun); the Yamuhakto, Warriors of the East and West; and the Koyemshi, or Mudheads, who act as clowns during the performances for the same reasons as the Koshares and Kurenas of Santo Domingo, in order to remind the people of their imperfections.

At Hopi there is a belief that the Kachinas emerged from the underworld with the people and lived with them so they could bring rain through the performance of their dances. But the people became disrespectful, and the Kachinas therefore departed and went off to live by themselves. They nevertheless told the people they would return each year, and masked Kachina dancers impersonate them in important ceremonies through which the prayers of the people are conveyed back

o the original Rainmakers. The Hopi have about thirty *mong*, or chief, Kachinas, and 250 or more other Kachinas who may appear at any time during the six-month Kachina season. The connection between the Kachinas, corn, rain, and other natural forces is beautifully summed up n this Korosta Kachina song, sung at corn-planting time when Kachinas wearing masks painted with the rainbow appear. These are compared vith pollen-painted butterflies as follows:

Yellow butterflies
Over the blossoming virgin corn,
With pollen-painted faces
Chase one another in brilliant throng.

Blue butterflies,
Over the blossoming virgin beans,
With pollen-painted faces
Chase one another in brilliant streams.
(Korosta Kachina song composed by Koianimptiwa)

LEFT:
The Pueblo Indians utilized natural forms to produce decorative artefacts and items of personal adornment. This necklace, made from seeds, is from Santo Domingo Pueblo.

ABOVE:
This pot, probably from Acoma, shows the distinctive polychrome geometric designs used by many Pueblo groups of the Southwest.

17

The Hopi year, like that of other Pueblo groups, is organized around a number of major annual ceremonies. The most important of these are Wuwuchim, Soyal, Powamu, and Niman. Wuwuchim is a re-enactment of the Hopi emergence myth, when the Two-Hearts caused dissension and fighting among the people and Sotuqnangu, the Sky God, in disgust, sent animals and birds to rescue the good people. The others he destroyed in terrifying floods. With the help of Shrike the good people emerged through Sipapu into the current world, where the deity Masau marked off the perimeters of the Hopi lands and gave them permission to settle there. A few Two-Hearts managed to escape the attentions of the One-Horned Priests who stayed below to prevent their emergence, and they are responsible for the strife and argument that still occur in a modern world.

Shortly after Wuwuchim, the Soyal Kachina appears in the Hopi villages. His walk is unsteady, as if he has just been reborn, and he sings in a quiet voice. Soyal appears in December, and this is the time to mark the rebirth of another year by planting sacred prayer sticks, or *pahos*. *Pahos* constitute a prayer to the ancestors and are made to encourage the fertility of animals, plants, and people, and to bless the houses they live in, as well as to bring rain; thus they may be used at other times of the year as well. A Zuni prayer made during the offering of *pahos* says:

The Southwest

RIGHT

This girl from Nambe Pueblo is shown wearing a blouse and a traditional wrap-around dress, or manta, *made from a rectangular piece of cloth which is folded under the left arm and pinned over the right shoulder. The pot she carries on her head is used for collecting water from one of the many natural and artificial reservoirs located near the Pueblo villages.*

BELOW

This pot probably comes from the Pueblo of Cochiti, where potters are known for their subtle and restrained use of black designs on a coloured slip.

This day I give you plume wands [pahos].
By means of your supernatural wisdom
You will clothe yourself with the plume wands.
Wherever you abide permanently,
Your little wind-blown cloud,
Your thin wisps of cloud,
Your hanging strips of cloud,
Your massed up clouds, replete with
living waters,
You will send forth to stay with us.
They will come standing on all sides.
With your fine rain caressing the earth,
With your weapons, the lightning,
With your rumbling thunder,
With your great crashes of thunder,
With your fine rain caressing the earth,
Your heavy rain caressing the earth,
With your great pile of waters here at Itiwana,
With these you will pass us on our roads;
In order that you may come to us thus
I have given you plume wands.
(Zuni prayer sung during the offerings of pahos to the
sacred ancestors at each full moon)

Powamu, commonly known as the Bean Dance, follows the Soyal and is the first major ceremony of the Kachina season. Most of the *mong*, or chief, Kachinas appear here, and it is at this ceremony that the majority of secondary Kachinas make their appearance. Beans are planted in the *kivas* and children are initiated into the cults, where they learn that the masked dancers are really human impersonators. During Powamu the Kachinas tour the villages and distribute presents – plaques, Kachina dolls, bows and arrows, rattles, moccasins – to the children who are too young to be initiated.

Niman, or Home Dance, marks the end of the Kachinas six-month stay among the Hopi. It coincides with the early harvest of corn and melons, which are distributed among the villagers and spectators, and the Kachinas who appear here tour the villages between dances giving out gifts. Corn bread, or *piki*, and other native foods are tossed to the crowds, and children receive rattles, toy bows and arrows, and miniature

FAR LEFT

Probably the most famous, and certainly one of the most implacable foes of the Europeans was the Apache shaman (medicine man) and war leader Geronimo. He is shown here in typical Apache dress of breechclout, loose shirt, and high moccasins. Note, too, the European jacket which would have been obtained either through trade or acquired as a war trophy.

LEFT

The Apache relied heavily on the intercession of supernaturals in their conflicts with both Native and European occupants of the Southwest area. This headgear, which may have been worn as a war cap, is painted with symbols that depict celestial forces and is decorated with hawk feathers that were believed to give warriors the ability to strike swiftly and unerringly.

LEFT

The Pueblo tribes and the Navaho quickly learned skills in metalworking and jewellery-making from itinerant Mexican traders. The bracelet shown here, inlaid with coal, turquoise, and coral on mother-of-pearl, is from Zuni Pueblo.

china dolls. During Niman the Kachinas may challenge the children a race, the loser being subjected to having his or her hair cut short and reby open to ridicule from their friends. In accordance with the eblo belief in harmony and balance, the Kachinas often lose the race.

Pueblo life, since it is based on a regular agricultural cycle, is rked by its stability and serenity, and it is this that has enabled the eblo groups to survive into the modern era with little change. though confronted by the demands of a modern world, most Pueblo ups have protected themselves by withdrawing and refusing to face pressures of imposed ideals and of an imposed economy. Many jor ceremonies, for example, are closed to all outsiders, including er Native Americans, to ensure that the integrity of Pueblo ritual life not disrupted.

Pima and Papago

ose to the Pueblo groups, and often described as 'circum-Pueblo', other ancient inhabitants of the desert Southwest. The principal ups among these are the related Pima and Papago, whose ancestors, Hohokam (Those Who Have Departed), had established self-fficient villages along the Gila and Salt Rivers to which some of the asazi (the Ancient Ones), from whom the modern Pueblos are scended, had fled to escape drought. The Hohokam welcomed these ugees, and archaeological records indicate that a number of mbined Hohokam-Anasazi villages existed in the past.

The Hohokam were successful agriculturalists who engineered the of river water through a system of irrigation ditches, dams, and ervoirs, and it was largely through their successful use of these ources that they could manage to support the Anasazi refugees. But aster struck. Raiding tribes from the east destroyed the Hohokam lages, and although they re-established themselves, further raids, lowed by prolonged droughts, finally broke the Hohokam economy d forced the groups to disperse into the modern Pima and Papago.

In more recent times the Pima and Papago have continued to lcome other groups into their midst. Refugee Apaches, even though Apaches were a sworn enemy, were accepted, as were remnants of Maricopa and Yuma, both of whom had waged wars against the na and Papago. The Pima and the Papago, like their ancestors the hokam, have a history of acceptance and non-aggression. When

challenged they fought bitterly; but they did not seek confrontation and, if left alone, were amiable neighbours. Their relations with whites, apart from a brief but insignificant interlude known as the 'Pima War', have been friendly and constructive.

According to the Papago, the world was created by Earthmaker and Buzzard, but was sewn together by the Spider People. Buzzard made the mountains and water courses, while Earthmaker was responsible for creating the stars, sun, and moon. Their first creation was imperfect, which resulted in a disagreement between Earthmaker, L'Itoi, and Coyote, and brought about a flood which destroyed these first people.

L'Itoi went underground and with the help of Wind secured the assistance of Gopher, who burrowed through the earth to create a hole from which the Pima and Papago could emerge. They established themselves in the desert after Gopher led them through four underworlds. Upon their emergence into this, the fourth world, they drove out their ancestors, the Hohokam, and established themselves in their place.

The Pima, however, place a greater emphasis on the work of Earth Magician in the creation of the world. With the help of the Ants, Earth Magician made a round ball of gum from the grease-wood stick he carried, and created the world by rolling this beneath his foot.

Earth Magician shapes this world.
Behold what he can do!
Round and smooth he moulds it.
Behold what he can do!
Earth Magician makes the mountains.
Heed what he has to say!
He it is that makes the mesas.
Heed what he has to say!
Earth Magician shapes this world;
Earth Magician makes its mountains;
Makes all larger, larger, larger.
Into the earth the Magician glances;
Into its mountains he may see.

Pima and Papago subsistence is based on limited agriculture, supplemented by hunting and the gathering of wild fruits, roots, and

OPPOSITE LEFT
In addition to the sedentary Pueblo tribes and the nomadic Apache and Navaho, the Southwest supported a number of circum-Pueblo groups whose life-style was based on a mixed economy of small-scale farming and hunting. These Pima women carry large baskets that were used to gather grain from fields that were maintained close to the village precincts.

OPPOSITE RIGHT
Early examples of Navaho weaving featured simple striped patterns arranged in bands of repeated designs, as shown in this classic example. Later blankets and rugs tend to be more complex in design and artificial aniline dyes rather than natural colours may have been used, although a revival in Navaho weaving after 1920 re-introduced vegetable dyes.

berries. The Papago, who have no access to any permanent water resources, spend from spring until autumn near the mouth of an *arroyo*, or channel of an intermittant stream, where flash floods water their crops. Since flood plains provide a precarious existence at best, the Papago are dependent on hardy desert plants that thrive under these

conditions, particularly the fruit of the giant saguaro cactus and the mesquite bean. The Pima, however, can rely on the permanence of the Gila River and its fertile farmlands and are therefore dependent on more stable cultivated crops.

Unlike the Pueblos, where corn, beans, and squash are part of the staple diet, perhaps four-fifths of Pima and Papago subsistence comes from non-agricultural pursuits, the Papago being more dependent on hunting and gathering than the Pima. Today, the Pima operate a community farm on the Gila River Reservation where they produce cotton. The Papago, by contrast, have gained a reputation as successful stock-raisers.

Both the Pima and Papago, nevertheless, have elaborate rituals intended to bring rain and the most powerful medicine men are those who are able to influence the weather. The importance of clouds, rain, thunder, lightning, and the rainbow is evident in this Pima song to the Swallow, the bringer of rain, which is sung at fiestas and dances:

Now the Swallow begins its singing;
Now the Swallow begins his singing.
And the women who are with me,
The poor women commence to sing.

The Swallows met in the standing cliffs;
The Swallows met in the standing cliffs.
And the rainbows arched above me,
There the blue rainbow arches met.

The history of the Pima and Papago is full of irony. Due to their refusal to involve themselves in dispute and their desire to live peaceably with their neighbours, they did not come into direct conflict with American forces, and as 'peaceful' subjects there was little reason for the United States to make treaties with them. The consequence of this is that they have been ignored in Anglo-Indian debate because there has been no legal basis for their claims to the lands they occupy. They were the last U.S. tribes to receive the right to vote, in 1949; the last to receive a permanent reservation, in 1906; and the last to receive mineral rights to their own lands, in 1959.

OPPOSITE
The Southwest provided many plant fibres and natural dyes that were extensively utilized in the production of baskets destined for a wide variety of uses. The basket shown on the left, bearing designs of human figures, is from the Apache; that on the right bears traditional abstract geometric designs typical of the Papago and which are said to represent the flow of water in Papago country.

LEFT
Navaho blankets and Apache 'conch' belt. The Southwest nurtured some of the most spectacular and distinctive forms of creative expression on the North American continent. Navaho blankets, with their bold colours and shapes, are unmistakable. The modern Apache belt, although using commercially manufactured silver conch discs, is nevertheless an equally distinctive form of Southwestern art.

Apache

The Apache are an enigma. They are presumed to have arrived in the Southwest shortly before the Spanish incursions, having migrated from the Subarctic areas of Canada; but the reasons for their migration and the date of their arrival in the Southwest are unknown and subject to much speculation. Even their name is curious, since the word Apache is a corruption of the Zuni Pueblo term for 'enemy'; yet there is little reason to suspect that the Zuni were particular enemies of the Apache groups. The Apache name for themselves is derived from Dine, the People, and may be pronounced as Inde, Tinneh, or Tinde, according to the dialect of the group.

Early records do not identify the Apache by name but refer only to wandering nomadic tribes, and although many of these may have been Apache families the identification is unclear. Yet it is certain that before the Spanish arrival the Apache had gained reputations as raiders in the area, and as early as 1598, only 50 years after the Spanish entry to the Southwest, they were well acquainted with the use of the horse, which the Spanish had reintroduced to North America and which the Apache raided from the Spanish rancherias. It is, in fact, likely that the dissemination of the horse from the rancherias of the Southwest to the Plains tribes in the north was largely due to raiding by the Apache tribes who then traded the horses to tribes living further north.

Although the Apache probably did not enter the Southwest much before 1200AD, they made their presence as fighters and warriors immediately felt and quickly gained reputations as fearless opponents when the Spanish, Mexicans, Texans, and Americans attempted to occupy their lands. Due to their implacable opposition, they became known as formidable enemies who would go to any length to defend Apacheria, the Apache homeland. The extent of Apache resistance is reflected in the fact that the names of their chiefs are recorded by the military authorities of the time. Cochise, Mangas Colorados, Victorio, and Geronimo are well known, simply because they resisted attempts to overrun Apacheria.

The fight to preserve their lands and their integrity was important to the Apache and should not be dismissed; yet the Apache themselves see things in a more positive light. For them, the world was created by Ysun, the Giver of Life, who has power over all living things. Ysun was assisted in his creation by White Painted Woman who 'existed from the beginning' and is the most important female deity in Apache mythology. Her sons (or in some versions her brothers) the Twin War Gods, Child of Water and Killer of Enemies, rid the world of the monsters, giants, dwarfs, and other forces that threatened the people's existence and left them with a country that was imbued with the life-giving powers of sun, moon, thunder, and lightning.

Thus the Apache concept is rooted in the sense of giving life, not of bringing death and destruction. But the original world was imperfect. Death was introduced, largely through the actions of Coyote, the Trickster, who also brought gluttony, thievery, adultery, and lying to the people. Apache relations with the whites with whom they fought and who attempted to occupy their lands are often reflected in the identification of the white man with the figure of Coyote.

To counteract the negative influence of Coyote, Ysun brought the Mountain and Water Beings into existence; but even Ysun was unable to deflect all the negative qualities. The Water Beings therefore consist of He Who Controls Water, a beneficial helper who always appears dressed in a shirt of many colours, and his counterpart, Water Monster, who can impart many positive qualities but, if angered, becomes an unpleasant and vindictive creature who inhabits lakes and pools and is responsible for deaths by drowning.

The Mountain People, by contrast, are the equivalent of the Kachinas of the Pueblos. Known as Gans, they once lived among the people but fled to the mountain tops to enjoy eternal life and to avoid the death that humans must suffer due to its introduction by Coyote. The Mountain People were instructed by White Painted Woman, and return each year during the important puberty rituals of Apache girls, when they come as healers and curers. Anyone treated by a girl who is under the influence of the Gans will enjoy a long, happy, and healthy life and will be ensured that the rest of their days will be spent walking on 'the pollen path'.

The pollen path was nevertheless interrupted by the explosion into Apacheria of other people. The beginning of this was in 1848, with the Treaty of Guadalupe Hidalgo that ended the Mexican war and placed New Mexico and Arizona in American hands. The Apache remained friendly with the Americans, whom they considered as 'friends' in their quarrels with the Mexicans. But in 1861 a local rancher, John Ward, complained that the Chiricahua, then under the leadership of Cochise, had stolen his cattle.

Cochise, suspecting nothing, arranged to meet the military commander, Lieutenant George Bascom, to discuss the issue; but Bascom, ignoring the fact that they were meeting under a flag of truce, attempted to arrest Cochise. Although Cochise escaped, his brother, two nephews, a woman, and two children who had innocently accompanied him, were arrested. Bascom, in fury at Cochise's escape, ordered the hanging of Cochise's relatives and thus began the Apache Wars.

This has to be considered in the light of the fact that in 1851 Cochise's father-in-law, Mangas Colorados, had addressed a party of commissioners investigating the 'Apache troubles', and had told them:

You came into our country. You were well-received. Your lives, your property, your animals, were safe. You passed by ones, by twos, by threes through our country. You went and came in peace. Your strayed animals were always brought home to you again. Our wives – our women and children – came here and visited at your houses. We were friends – we were brothers! Believing that we were brothers and that you would feel as we feel, we concealed nothing. We came not secretly nor in the night. We came in open day, and before your faces. We believed your assurances of friendship, and we trusted them.

Shortly after making this speech, during a friendly visit to a mining camp, Mangas Colorados was stripped, tied to a post, and given a severe whipping – intended as a lesson to the Apache that they should remain subservient, but an insult that few people could be expected to tolerate. A few years later, during an abortive attempt to secure a truce, another young Apache, Geronimo, was deceived and a number of Geronimo's family were kidnapped and executed. Such betrayals incensed the Apache, who started a campaign of resistance. The kidnapping of Apache boys as slaves and the forced prostitution of Apache girls served to inflame the situation.

Cochise, together with Mangas Colorados, resisted American attempts to destroy the Apache, but in 1863 Mangas Colorados unwisely accepted an invitation to peace talks in an attempt to resolve the problem. He arrived at the army camp on Pinos Altos on 17 January 1863, when he was immediately seized. The governing officer, General West, made it clear he wanted Colorados caught 'dead or alive', emphasizing the word 'dead', and during the night the army sentries, by heating their bayonets in the camp fire and then pressing them against Mangas's feet ensured

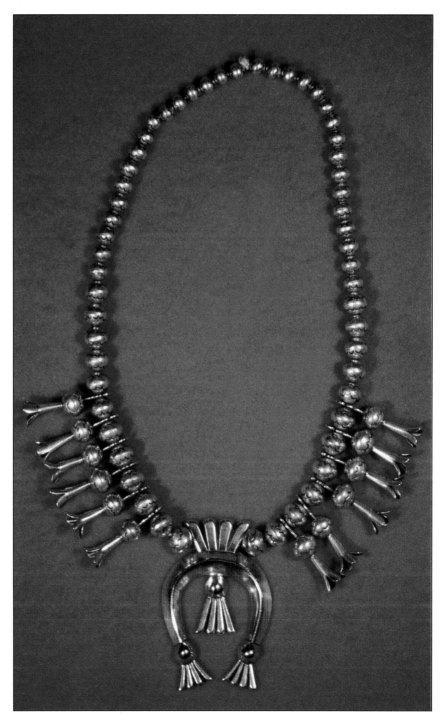

Although the Apache and Navaho are linguistically closely related, it was only the Navaho who adopted a semi-sedentary life-style and fully-developed skills in weaving and jewellery-making. The Navaho 'squash blossom' necklace shown here is a classic example of a traditional design that has been used by the Navaho since their first contact with the Spanish.

The Southwest

that their captive leapt up in pain and was shot dead in what was explained as an attempt to escape.

Surprisingly, Cochise managed to avert an all-out war with the Americans, and in 1872 agreed to the establishment of Apache reservations in the Chiricahua homelands and to protect settlers and other whites travelling through Apache Pass. He kept his word, and the Chiricahua remained peaceful until Cochise's death in 1874. But other Apache, infuriated at the treatment they were receiving, proved less tractable. Victorio, who had grown up under the leadership of Mangas Colorados, led his Mimbreno Apache in a relentless war against the Americans from 1877 to 1880.

Geronimo, who had fought with Cochise and is perhaps the most famous of Apache chiefs, rallied his band of Chiricahua and fought against the United States between 1881 and 1886. Apache resentment stemmed from long years of bitter contact with the Spanish, the Mexicans, and now the Americans. Geronimo recalled his feelings when, in 1852, on returning from a hunting party, he found that his wife, his three children, and his widowed mother had been killed by Mexican troops from Sonora:

> *Without being noticed I silently turned away and stood by the river. How long I stood there I do not know. Our chief, Mangas Colorados, gave the order to start at once in perfect silence for our homes in Arizona, leaving the dead. I stood still until all had passed, hardly knowing what I would do – I had no weapon, nor did I hardly wish to fight, nor did I contemplate recovering the bodies of my loved ones, for that was forbidden. I did not pray, nor did I resolve to do anything in particular, for I had no purpose left. I finally followed the tribe in silence, keeping just within hearing distance of the soft noise of their feet.*

By 1874 all the hostile Apache groups had officially been rounded up, with the help of General Crook's 'friendly' Apache scouts, and placed on reservations; but Geronimo's Chiricahua, together with some Mogollon, Mimbres, and Coyotero Apache, continued raiding into Mexico.

It was not until 1886 that Geronimo's handful of warriors – by now totalling only 24 against an American army of 5,000 – was finally persuaded to surrender. They, together with the Apache scouts who had helped locate the mountain strongholds of the 'hostiles', and in complete disregard of General Nelson Miles's assurances that they would be given a

servation in Apacheria, were sent in chains to Fort Pensacola in Florida prisoners-of-war. They were relocated from there to Mount Vernon arracks, Alabama, where about a quarter of the Apache died from berculosis and other diseases. Although it was clear that the Apache had be moved for humanitarian reasons, they were refused re-entry by the tizens of Arizona and were instead removed to Fort Sill, Oklahoma, here Geronimo died in 1909, far from the lands in which his relatives d been buried.

Today the Apache, who now live on reservations in New Mexico and rizona, continue to practise many of their old ceremonies but subsist on oney derived from stock-raising, leases to timber and mineral rights, or urist income. San Carlos, in eastern Arizona, is the largest of the serves and is primarily timber and cattle country, whereas the White fountain Apache at Fort Apache, also in Arizona, own the largest dependent recreation area in the western United States with over 300 iles of trout streams and lakes.

Despite their dependence on outside income, the Apache continue to voke their ancient deities. Among the Western Apache, the Gans appear very year to celebrate the girls' puberty rites, when they re-enact their escent from the mountains and bring blessings to the people. In night-me dances, illuminated by huge fires, the Gans suddenly appear from orth, east, south, and west, wearing headdresses emblazoned with epictions of lightning and of the stars, while among the Eastern groups e red and white clans meet annually in a foot race by a sacred lake to etermine which of them will be responsible for the security of the tribe r the forthcoming year.

Navaho

When the Spanish first arrived in the Southwest they met a group of Apache Indians living in the vicinity of an abandoned Pueblo known as Navahú (Great Fields) and accordingly named them L'Apaches de Navahú.

Although originally little different from other Apache groups, the Navaho were more readily prepared to adopt influences from the different tribes with whom they came in contact. This resulted in a revolution in Navaho life-style and economy. They quickly acquired skills in weaving, pottery and jewellery-making, and farming, and became sheep-herders and raisers rather than using the animals exclusively as a food source as other Apache groups had done.

Although Navaho life is pastoral and based on sheep-herding, the roots of Apache nomadism go deep and Navaho homes or *hogans* are widely scattered; to visit a neighbour requires a journey. In the beginning, when the Navaho world was being created, Dawn Boy established the pattern of movement by singing:

In the house of long life,
There I wander.
In the house of happiness,
There I wander.
Beauty before me,
With it I wander.
Beauty behind me,
With it I wander.
Beauty below me,
With it I wander.
Beauty above me,
With it I wander.
Beauty all around me,
With it I wander.
In old age travelling,
With it I wander.
On the beautiful trail I am,
With it I wander.

Dawn Boy, the child of First Man and First Woman, travelled to the Navaho country on a sunbeam and moved from mountain to mountain by standing on a rainbow. He defined the Navaho country by placing a

LEFT
Turquoise was much prized by the Southwestern tribes and much of it was originally mined locally. Since then, many of the seams of local turquoise have given out and modern jewellery-makers rely on the use of imported turquoise from China which has a more greenish colour. This Navaho ring, made from local turquoise, uses a single nugget more than $1\frac{1}{2}$ inches (4cm) in diameter. Note how the natural shape of the turquoise has been retained and incorporated into the silver mounting of the ring.

sacred mountain at the east which was made from white shell, fastened to the earth by a bolt of lightning and covered with a sheet of daylight. In the south was a mountain made from turquoise, fastened with a knife of stone and covered with blue sky. To the west he placed a mountain of abalone that he fastened to the earth with a sunbeam and covered with a yellow cloud. And in the north he placed a mountain of jet that was fastened with a rainbow and covered in darkness.

Having defined the perimeters of the Navaho country, the people were then allowed to emerge through a hollow reed and were placed on Tsichlnaodichcli, the striped agate mountain, which is at the centre of the Navaho world. Before naming the mountains, the Holy People sang songs telling of their journeys, and gave these Hozhonji, or Holy Songs, to the people. Such songs should always be used before starting a journey and in any appeals to the deities. These are songs of peace which protect the people against all evil, and every ceremony ends with one since it is the final blessing.

The Hozhonji have even greater significance, however, since it is through them that the entire Navaho world was brought into being and kept in balance and harmony. Whenever these songs are sung, the singer's spirit makes the journey the songs describe. He is said to travel on a rainbow from mountain to mountain, for this is the way the deities travel, and each mountain symbolizes the essence of Navaho belief. The mountain is pure and holy, 'there is freedom above it, freedom below it, freedom all around it', and the songs are always sung in the order of east, south, west, and north, since this is the way the sun moves.

Singing Hozhonji makes man like the mountain, pure and holy, eternally blessed. Through the songs people are restored to health and are able to 'walk in beauty', in accordance with the principles that were established by the Holy People when the world was created. Often the songs are sung as part of elaborate curing rituals that may take several days to complete and which, according to Navaho belief, must be performed to perfection. Any mistake in any part of the ritual or the singing would render the cure ineffective.

Associated with the cures and singing are complex sand-paintings, diagrammatic drawings made on the ground with coloured sands and depicting events in the mythical episodes to which the songs refer. The concept of perfection and movement is again apparent here; by seating the patient on the sand-painting any illness, weakness, or lethargy is transferred from the patient to the painting, which is then erased so that negative force can be dissipated and sent into a void where it is rendered harmless, thus restoring balance and harmony.

All Navaho ceremony and ritual is intended to restore this original harmony, and the spiritual journey to the mountains which occurs through the songs and cures is conceived as a 'homecoming': a return to the 'Chief of all mountains' and to happiness and peace.

Navaho ideals of beauty and happiness were nevertheless disrupted in the 1860s, when a military force under Colonel Kit Carson was dispatched to subdue the tribe. Carson did not confront the Navahos directly, but instead employed a policy of destroying their economic basis. Livestock was slaughtered, fields of corn and pumpkins were destroyed, and the extensive peach orchards of the Canyon de Chelly were cut down. Starved into submission, the Navaho surrendered and were forced into confinement on the Bosque Redondo Reservation at Fort Sumner on the Pecos River in southeastern New Mexico, hundreds of miles from their homelands.

The surrender of some 8,000 Navaho men, women, and children, is the largest single capitulation in the history of the United States; but conditions at Bosque Redondo were dreadful. Crops failed, the water was bad, there was a shortage of firewood, and infestations of insects had devastating results. More than 2,000 Navaho died from disease and starvation after their 'Long Walk' to captivity. In 1868 the survivors were finally permitted to return home since it was considered cheaper to allow them their freedom than to keep them in confinement.

Surprisingly, the Navaho re-established themselves, prospered, and grew in numbers. Today they are the largest tribe in the United States and are famed for the silver-and-turquoise jewellery and the blankets they produce. Once again, myth and movement is incorporated into the design and patterns the Navaho employ, since it is said that turquoise was given them by Changing-Woman and that Spider-Woman taught them how to weave. The first blanket woven by Spider-Woman was made from lightning and sunbeams, and every blanket or rug is said to reflect this original concept.

Though famed for these crafts, neither of them is original to the Navaho. The Navaho used precious metals to adorn bridles from the time of Spanish contact, but it was not until about 1850 that silverworking was learned from the Mexicans. By 1870, however, a distinctive Navaho style

It is an unfortunate fact that most Navaho blankets are today seen as decorative objects, to be displayed on the walls of museums or in the homes of private collectors, when they are seen as flat objects. The designs on Navaho blankets are nevertheless intended to be 'animated', as seen in this example of a folded child's blanket.

The Southwest

Woven sashes are traded widely in the Southwest and are familiar items of women's ceremonial costume. Modern examples, such as the one shown here, use re-spun commercial yarns for the warp to produce slightly raised designs in red and black, which are wrapped around an invisible weft of cotton string.

had already emerged. Weaving, too, was borrowed from elsewhere. Sheep were introduced to the Southwest by the Spanish, and the Navaho learned weaving skills from the Pueblo tribes, again developing a highly distinctive style of their own.

Although most early Navaho blankets are now collectors' items – and a good early 19th-century one recently sold at auction for half a million dollars, the highest price ever reached for a single item of Native American tribal art – the Navaho concept was never that they should be displayed on the walls of museums or of wealthy collectors. They were made to be worn and seen in motion, and the brilliant patterns and colours are said to be expressive of the power of Navaho origins.

The unpredictable weather conditions of the Southwest meant that foods harvested in autumn had to be stored for winter use. This Apache basket, used for storing grain, is over 3ft (1m) in height and when filled would have been left in a dry cave or other shelter so that people returning to a winter campsite could help themselves.

California

OPPOSITE LEFT

The Mohave of the southern Arizona-California area were known for their use of facial markings, or tattoos, that indicated female status and family lineage. This Mohave pottery doll, decorated with beads, string, trade cloth, and plant fibres, clearly shows facial markings.

OPPOSITE RIGHT

The southern Californian tribes were missionized by the Spanish at an early date and quickly lost any sense of tribal identity. The men and women shown in this photograph taken in the 1880s, and despite the fact that the men are wearing traditional face and body paint, are identified merely as 'Diegueños': that is, Indians belonging to the mission of San Diego. The women, presumably to conform to European notions of modesty, are dressed in blankets and shawls rather than the short apron that would formerly have been worn.

Although comprising only about 1 per cent of the North American land mass, California supported in excess of 10 per cent of the aboriginal population. A moderate climate, an abundance of game and fish and numerous roots, fruits, and berries in season, all served to sustain the small tribal groups that made up California's inhabitants.

In some ways it was an ideal land. Thriving on the resources they found there, the Californians needed little else and there was no need for competition since land and sea provided everything they required. As a consequence, the tribal groups lived peaceably side by side, warfare was unknown, and no weapons – either offensive or defensive – were employed by any of them.

It was a healthy and invigorating climate. When Europeans first arrived they were astonished at the beauty of the women and the strength and dexterity of the men. A Californian man was said to be able to run for a mile or more with a load that a European could hardly lift from the ground. But such an idyllic world – referred to as 'Paradise' in early reports – was not destined to last.

Spanish explorers, travelling north from Mexico, easily subdued the non-aggressive Californian Indians and founded missions that were intended to 'civilize' the natives. They herded these passive peoples together and subjected them to a régime of captivity and incarceration that has few parallels elsewhere in the world. The extent of Spanish dominance is reflected in Californian place names: San Francisco, San Jose, Santa Cruz, San Luis Obispo, Santa Maria, Santa Barbara, Los Angeles, Santa Ana, and San Diego are all names of Spanish missions that were established between 1769 and 1823.

Conditions at the missions were abysmal. The Indians were forced to have their hair shorn, denied any sense of an Indian identity, forbidden to speak their own languages, and were put to work manufacturing goods that the Spanish desired but which were of little relevance to any of the native economies. Apart from daily bible readings, the main tasks of the Mission Indians were the production of furniture, shoes, candles, and soap, and the maintenance of orchards, gardens, pasturelands, and granaries.

So effective was Spanish rule that few of the groups remain as tribal entities. From San Diego to San Francisco we know of them merely as Mission Indians, and even the tribal names that have survived – such as Diegueño or Luiseño – refer to the missions rather than to original tribal groups. Yet despite the manner in which Spanish beliefs were imposed, their intent was essentially humane – to educate and Christianize the 'heathens'.

This was to change when California passed into American hands and the missions were abandoned. Although released from the missions and returned to their homelands, little tribal government remained and the authority of the chiefs and shamans had been broken. Many of the homelands were occupied by white ranchers, who were reluctant to give up the easy Californian way of life to ex-Mission Indians. Instead, they 'employed' the Indians under conditions of servitude even more severe than those that had applied in the missions.

Then, in the 1840s, gold was discovered in California and the state's white population escalated. It increased almost ten-fold within a few

years. The gold-seekers had little respect for the white ranchers whose lands they invaded, and even less for the Indians they found living there. If Indians occupied lands on which gold had been found, the simplest expedient was to poison or shoot them. The law gave little or no protection to vulnerable Indian groups, and entire tribes disappeared under the onslaught of the white invaders of their territories.

The Mission Tribes

In 1602, Spanish ships commanded by Vizcaino called at Santa Catalina and Monterey, where they came into contact with the Indians of California. They noted the 'fairness and beauty' of the Californian women, but, apart from a few brief days of trade, did not remain long enough to make their presence felt.

California was left at peace until 1697, when Jesuit missionaries established themselves in the area, where they were to remain until expelled by Charles III of Spain in 1767. Then, following the expulsion of the Jesuits and primarily driven by the need to establish a refitting point for their galleons, Spain established the Mission of San Diego in 1769. A number of local tribes – including the Kamia, Ipai, and Tipai – were herded together at the mission and are known today as the Diegueños. In the years between the founding of San Diego and 1823, a total of 21 missions were built. These had religious, political, and economic significance, and were under the authority of Franciscan priests protected by soldiers from nearby presidios.

For the Indian tribes occupying California, from San Francisco southwards, the missions were disastrous. Peace-loving, and with little tribal authority or government, the tribes offered little resistance and were easy prey to the Spanish. They quickly capitulated and individual tribal identities were lost.

Prior to the Spanish arrivals, the tribes of southern California had lived peaceably side by side. Everything they required could be obtained locally and there was little need for exploration and expansion. Even trade between neighbouring tribes was limited, since there was no need to exchange or barter for goods. The only trading that occurred was between groups living on the coast and interior tribes, when products of the sea, such as shells, were exchanged for those of the inland forests. Life was thus lived within a restricted locality, and there were few, if any, migration legends or tales of travel. People simply believed they

originated where they now lived, although they often credited this to some supernatural power or deity who brought them into being:

> *I am in this world*
> *I travel in the air*
> *I was not born in the earth*
> *I was born in the sky*
> *My father is the North Cloud*
> *My mother, the South Cloud.*

> *I have come to call you from the ocean.*
> *You will be needed in this world.*
> *When trees come, you will quicken them.*
> *When people come, you will comfort them.*
> *You will make the life of the people.*
> *Do not refuse me*
> *I am not deceiving you.*
> (Annikadel, C. Hart Merriam)

The emphasis placed on the Cloud Beings in the above is characteristic of southern Californian belief. The majestic Californian condor was revered as a messenger of the sky powers, and elaborate sand-paintings depicting the movements of the stars, and which acted as lunar-solar calendars, were made by the shamans.

Shamans were, perhaps, the most influential force among the southern Californians, due, in part, to the lack of a strong chieftainship. People looked to the shamans for guidance and advice as well as for leadership, and events of a shamanic nature were of importance to all. Of major importance among these was the Toloache, or Datura, cult of initiation, which every adolescent undertook as a rite of passage from childhood to maturity.

During the Toloache, ingestions of the vision-inducing datura (Jimson weed) were taken to produce vivid hallucinatory dreams that were said to influence an individual's mystic and religious thought throughout his or her life. During such dreams, the Great Ones – the ancient inhabitants of the land and the creators of 'things-as-they-are-now' – would visit the dreamer and impart knowledge. In fact, all knowledge stemmed from the Great Ones, including the powers that the shamans possessed.

Why the Great Ones chose to give up their earthly home and leave

LEFT
Alice Spott, the daughter of a wealthy Hupa leader, is shown standing here in front of a traditional split-plank house and wearing an abundance of shell necklaces and shell-decorated clothing that signify family status.

BELOW
Although most of the Californian tribes excelled in basketmaking, the Pomo achieved an enviable reputation for their manufacture of exquisite gift baskets decorated with brightly-coloured feathers and shell pendants. Such baskets served no practical purpose and were intended to honour an important guest and to serve as an indication of the maker's skill.

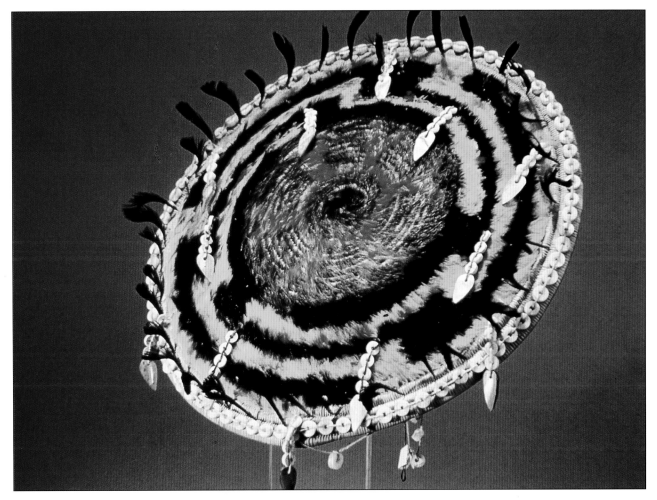

California

RIGHT
Heinmot Tooyalaket, or Chief Joseph, of the Nez Percé was an exceptional leader who always sought to maintain peace between his tribe and white intruders and settlers in Nez Percé lands. Eventually, white depredations resulted in Indian reprisals and the enforced flight of the tribe in an attempt to seek refuge in Canada. After many miles of desperate travel in severe winter weather, characterized by what has been described as Joseph's 'magnificent military strategy', the destitute Nez Percé were finally stopped just 50 miles (80km) from the safety of the Canadian border.

BELOW RIGHT
Passive resistance to white incursions and influence was nowhere more apparent than by the Seri of southern California, who refused all trade contacts and even in recent years refused to use metal tools or other goods introduced by white traders. Candelaria, the Seri girl depicted here, bears the traditional face painting that depicts her family lineage.

they had made, they said farewell' to the people they had created. But although bidding the people farewell, the Great Ones gave them access to their powers whenever the need arose. According to the Luiseño (the Indians of the Mission of San Luis Obispo:

> *The earth hears you.*
> *The sky and the sacred mountain see you.*
> *If you will believe this you will grow old,*
> *And you will see your sons and daughters*
> *And you will counsel them in this manner*
> *When you reach your old age.*

(Song sung during Luiseño initiation ceremonies)

it to the people is never fully explained. Usually, it was at the instigation of one of the more powerful of them, often the Creator himself, who persuaded the others to retreat to the sky or to turn themselves into other creatures or natural forms. Butterflies, lizards – even springs and waves – all contain the power of one or more of the Great Ones that has been left behind for the people's benefit.

Within these powers there is combined the happiness of creativity as well as the sadness of departure, since the Great Ones left behind them an emotional response to the forces of the land they had created. Most tales suggest they realized that to co-exist with the people would cause disharmony and strife. It is said that 'sadly, because they loved the world

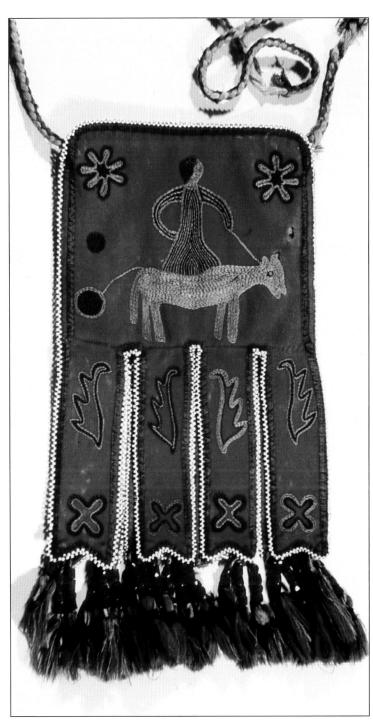

FAR LEFT
The Klikitat of the Cascades region of British Columbia and Washington made exquisite baskets from spruce-root and bear grass using an imbrication technique that was unique to this region. In this, each coil that forms the base of the basket is covered with a strip of coloured grass or bark that is sewn in place beneath the coil to produce a 'tiled' effect.

LEFT
Highly characteristic of the Plateau tribes, such as the Thompson River tribes and the Nez Percé, were so-called 'octopus' bags, named after the tentacle-shaped fringe. The reputation of these tribes as horse breeders and traders is indicated in the motif used to decorate the bag shown here.

California

OPPOSITE
Communal dances, sponsored by wealthy
members of the village, were an important aspect
of Californian life and included the display of
elaborate items of costume that indicated status,
such as the headbands decorated with
woodpecker scalps worn by these dancers. They
were photographed at the Yurok town of Pekwon
on the Klamath River in 1893.

Central California

Often considered to be the 'typical' Californian Indian, and comprising well over half the total population of California, the Indians of the central regions had similar beliefs in the powers of the Creative Gods and a strong faith in shamanism though they had also developed more clearly defined systems of leadership and of political authority. The Yuma say:

You know how some men are quick and strong and know the things to do, how people like to do things for them, and how they have a gift for getting everybody cheerful? Well, those men were kwoxot – tribal leaders.

The Yuma reference to one of the functions of the chief being to make 'everybody cheerful' is an interesting point, since among them and other tribes of the central regions, such as the Yokut, Wintu, Maidu, and Pomo, the chief, or headman, had no power or authority other than that the people liked and trusted him and respected his opinion. He would be consulted in any dispute or quarrel and his word was acted upon simply because it was known that he bore no malice and had everyone's best interests at heart.

Like the southern groups, those of the central area also saw war in a negative light, and this, again, is reflected in the role of the headman. Regardless of his age or fighting ability he would never become physically involved in a dispute, neither within the village nor with any neighbouring groups. War, though only ever engaged in reluctantly, was nevertheless recognized as a necessary evil, since disputes could occur. At such times the war party, most usually a group of relatives since disputes in the region were often family feuds, was led by a person especially appointed for the occasion.

The chief, by remaining neutral, was able to negotiate with the equally neutral chief of a neighbouring group in the event of hostilities occurring, and between them they would attempt to resolve the argument. This was usually determined by assessing the damage both sides had suffered and arranging for indemnity to be paid in the form of *kaia* – strings of dentalium shells that had a fixed value according to their length, and which acted as a form of currency.

In line with Californian notions of fairness and equality, it was often agreed that both sides should compensate each other, thereby ensuring that neither party would feel they had been unfairly treated and at the conclusion of the unpleasant interlude the disputants would come together

for a celebratory dance. This was not intended to applaud acts of violence but was to rejoice in the fact that such acts were at an end and that life could continue in its usual unaggressive and unhurried manner.

Inter-village hostilities were unusual in that each tribe had a clearly defined territory and rarely ventured beyond it. When Earth-Maker and Great-Grandfather created the world they gave specific homes to the different tribes. It is said that Earth-Maker breathed life into the First People and then

he gave homes to them, some in a fold of the hills, others by the sea. To each he said, 'Here is your home and the home of the children who will be born to you. Your land reaches from here to here.' So saying he indicated a place upstream and one downstream, also the crest of the first line of hills and a tall pine or a boulder or other marker to show the boundaries beyond which the land belonged to someone else.

Social control within the village itself was more often expressed by voicing disapproval, designed to embarrass the offender into mending his or her ways, than by any form of physical punishment or sanction. In such closely-knit communities, where people rarely ventured far beyond the immediate vicinity of the village, disapproval was a very effective means of ensuring adherence to the ethical and practical needs of the village as a whole.

In cases of severe disagreement or discontent, however, or if an argument had developed to the point where a fellow villager had been killed, banishment from the tribe was the ultimate penalty. By removing the cause of the trouble, peaceful co-existence would be ensured. Banishment was nevertheless rare and never undertaken lightly, and the decision could not be taken by the headman alone. A council was held to which every adult member of the village was invited, including the accused, and at which the individual merits of the case were debated and discussed. Thus banishment could only occur with the agreement of the entire village.

More usually, punishment for any transgression was made through payment of compensation, in much the same way that warfare was formally terminated. The offender would be ordered to pay the requisite amount of *kaia* to recompense the aggrieved party, the amount again depending on agreement reached through discussion and general debate. *Kaia*, in fact, appears as a structuring and controlling device for

California

numerous aspects of central Californian life.

If dances were to be held, any families that had recently been bereaved and were still in mourning would be paid in *kaia*, donated by the wealthy members of the tribe, to 'buy' their sorrow. Insults were 'buried' through payments of *kaia*, strangers were welcomed with gifts of *kaia* or with beautifully decorated miniature baskets hung with feathers, beads, and *kaia* strings, and marriages were solemnized by the exchange of *kaia*.

The Californian desire to avoid conflict and resolve disputes by any means other than by physical intervention was recorded by early European visitors to this area, who described the people as '*shy and reserved in contact with strangers although very courteous ... they express a wish for gentleness, amiability, and stability.*' This wish was expressed in every aspect of central Californian life. The centre of the village was the men's house, where boys received training and instruction from the elders of the village, and the women's house, where young girls were taught basketmaking and other feminine skills by the older women.

Although the family was important, central Californian life centred on the community. Food was communally shared and any summer surplus was stored in baskets and set aside to feed the entire village in the event of winter shortages. Every member of the village met regularly to discuss matters of importance, and children were welcomed into any house they cared to visit and were considered to be the responsibility of the village as a whole rather than the sole responsibility of their parents. Elder Uncle, speaking to his nephews and nieces, says:

See these old men and women: they paid attention to this counsel which is of grown-up people, and they have already reached old age. One must respect his elders, listen to them, give them food freely, not eat meals secretly, refrain from anger, be cordial and polite ... You must not look sideways, must not receive a person in your house with anger ... Pay attention to this speech and as your son or daughter grows up, you will bathe in water, and your hair will grow long and you will not feel cold, and you will be fat. Do not neglect to paint yourself, and people will see, and you will grow old.

Even the shamans, who were known to possess powers whereby they could send magic arrows over the hills to attack and destroy their enemies, were more renowned for their healing gifts than for any negative force they might control. Some were able to diagnose disease, others able to cure it. Again, there is a sharing of responsibility and a knowledge that each individual is prepared and willing to exchange wisdom and advice. A Wintu prayer, sung to the ghosts of the departed, reflects the positive attitude of the central Californian Indians:

From the old camping place
Comes a flash of flowers.
I love flowers.
Give me flowers.
Flowers flutter
As the wind raises them above.
I love flowers.
Give me flowers.
(Wintu: *Song of a Ghost*)

Northern California

The tribes of northern California, the Yurok, Karok, Hupa, Modoc, and Klamath, shared the characteristics of other Californian groups but placed even greater emphasis on status and wealth. Family rights to the use of hunting and fishing territories and to stands of oak and other timbers were strongly defended, unlike the communal holdings that pertained further south. Individual wealth and personal gain were cherished ideals, and although there was no rank order in ceremonies or other communal gatherings, it is nevertheless clear that in some respects personal accomplishment was considered more important than community need.

The importance of the individual is reflected in this Modoc dream song:

I stand on the rim of my nest.
I am enveloped in flames.
What am I? What am I?
I, the song, I walk here.

Assessment of an individual's worth was based on his ability to pay the full purchase price for a bride from the most virtuous family, to own a house with a good name and in a good area, to be able to demonstrate wealth in the form of many strings of *kaia*, and to possess elaborate dance costumes and flicker tail-feather headdresses that could be

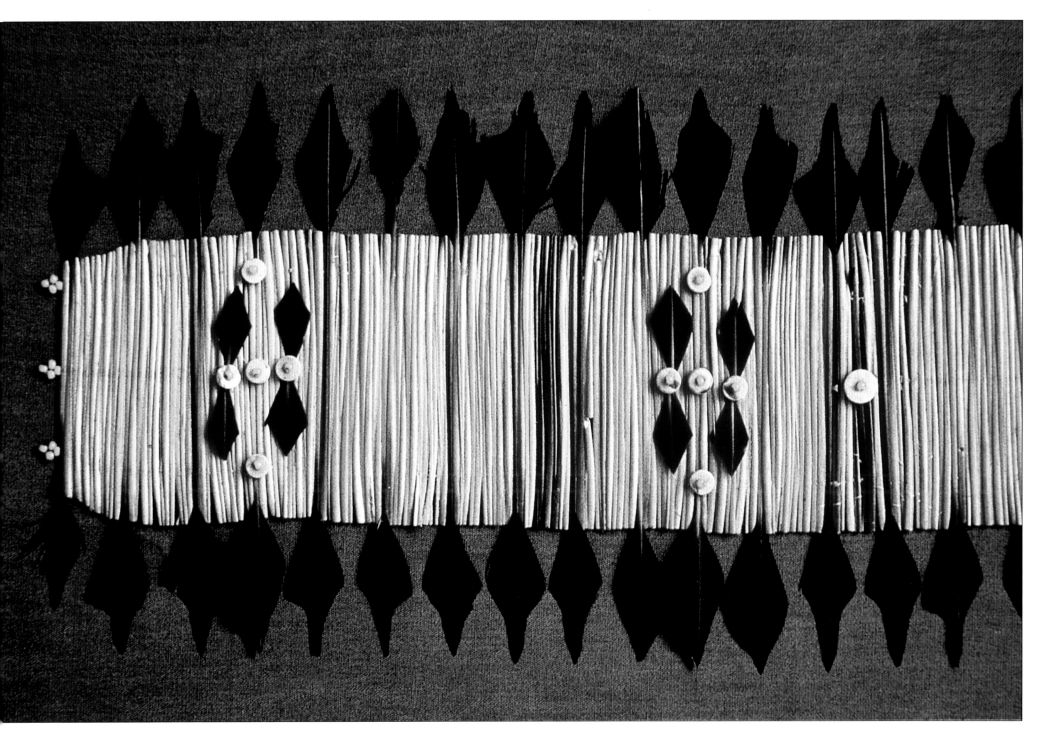

California

Traditional women's headgear in the northern California area was the basketry cap, such as this Hupa example. Such caps were worn by the wives and daughters of wealthy men whenever they appeared in public and were symbols of the family's status as well as of the women's skill in weaving.

displayed during important ceremonies. So important were these that wealthy families kept carved wooden chests full of such 'treasures', which could be opened at public events.

Incumbent upon these wealthy families, however, was the necessity for them to act as hosts during public displays, since it was their social duty to finance dances – which included feasting all the participants – which might last as long as three weeks. In return for this, the family head held a position of prestige within the community. In this respect northern Californian headmen were hereditary leaders, holding that position because of the family's acquired wealth, rather than as respected wise men who enjoyed the trust of their fellow tribesmen.

There was nevertheless a sense of wholeness, in morality, ethics, and belief that was unchanging and constant. A tale told a hundred times and known to all was appreciated for its familiarity, and the leading families, who had held their positions for generations, were respected as if appointed by the Creator Gods when they first brought the world into being. Therefore the will of the Gods, nature, the spirit world, and that of the people were inextricably intertwined and bound together, and everything that happened in the 'real' world was locked into explanations that could be found in the myths and stories told by the elders.

Thus an earthquake happened because a giant who slept beneath the earth rolled over in his sleep, and an eclipse of the sun was merely one of the Sky Monsters attempting to devour it. The northern Californians knew that the Sky Monsters would be defeated just as surely as they knew that their own leaders would prevail against any opposition from outside the tribe. Thus the 'Way' – the right manner in which people should live and the values they should uphold, as well as the choices, possibilities, and decisions that needed to be made – was defined by the Creator Gods and unambiguously fixed in the lives of the people.

Great Basin Tribes

Contiguous to, and sometimes grouped with, the Californian tribes are those of the desert lands of Utah, Nevada, and southern Oregon. Like the Californians they were referred to in early reports as 'Digger Indians' due to their reliance on the gathering of edible roots and tubers and like them were peace-loving groups who lived in what were essentially extended family groups.

The deserts, however, were unable to support the relatively easy sedentary life-style of the Californians. Resources – including edible roots, game animals, and water – were extremely scarce and widely scattered, and this forced the groups into living nomadically, since it was essential for them to move about to avoid depleting the few resources existing in any single area.

Scarcity of resources also prevented them from forming permanent tribes, and although recognizing their affinity to groups speaking the same or similar languages each 'tribe' was, in effect, a scattered handful of family bands, possibly numbering only a dozen or so people, which met together for tribal celebrations for only a few days of the year.

Since virtually all their time was spent gathering food or hunting

The Nez Percé of the Plateau region were famed as horse traders, but were also renowned for their exceptional skill in weaving bags such as this one made from the inner parts of corn husks. Similar bags were also woven from bear grass, although this practice had been superseded by the use of corn husks before the close of the 19th century.

California

Klikitat basketry was recognized throughout the Plateau region as being superior in design and execution, and was often used as a standard trade item in their interactions with other tribes. The basket shown here uses a characteristic imbrication technique and depicts five standing figures. The reverse, not shown, utilizes darker grasses to form a double row of interlocking diamonds.

small game, such as rabbits, the arts of the area were little developed. Some basketry was made as well as blankets of rabbit fur. Yet, perhaps surprisingly, it was from this unpromising land that the last swell of uprising and protest against American occupation stemmed, in the form of the Ghost Dance of the 1890s.

The Paiute Ghost Dance

The Ghost Dance was inspired by the vision of a Paiute shaman named Wovoka, who dreamed of a great flood that destroyed the Whites and of the return to earth of all dead Indians and of the buffalo. It was a messianic vision which spread rapidly to the tribes of the Great Plains to the east of the Basin area, who by now were penned up on reservations and reliant on government hand-outs since the mainstay of their economy, the buffalo, had been wiped out.

Although the Ghost Dance on the Plains was to lead to violent confrontations, Wovoka's vision, in keeping with Basin beliefs, was a peaceful one. It merely required the Indians to dance until exhausted when they would fall into a trance and dream of their loved ones who were soon to return. As Wovoka himself explained it:

Grandfather [the Messiah] *says, when your friends die you must not cry. You must not hurt anybody or do harm to anyone. You must not fight. Do right always. It will give you satisfaction in life. The dead are all alive again. I do not know when they will be here; maybe this fall or in the spring. When the time comes there will be no more sickness and everyone will be young again. Do not make any trouble ... when the earth shakes do not be afraid. It will not hurt you.*

(Wovoka, Paiute shaman, 1889)

Plateau Tribes

the more fertile areas of northern Oregon, part of Washington, and aho, lived a group of small tribes who form a transition between the e-styles of California and the Great Basin, and those of the Great ains to their east and of the Northwest Coast to their west.

The best known of these tribes are the Cayuse and the Nez Percé, due their later development of selective horse-raising which led to the stinctive dappled Indian pony, or Appaloosa, and because of the dramatic ght of the Nez Percé in an attempt to elude U.S. troops and escape from hite oppression into Canada. There were numerous other small tribal oups, among them the Wishram and Wasco, Lillooet, Thompson, huswap, Coeur d'Alene, Flathead, and the tribes of the Fraser Valley.

In contrast to the Great Basin, the Plateau is river country, and though sharing the Californian and Great Basin dependency on bsistence gathering, and with no agriculture or farming, they also relied eavily on products of the rivers. Fish, particularly trout and sturgeon, were important food source for all the tribes, and in some areas salmon were entiful at certain times of the year, and fresh, dried, or smoked salmon as a major part of the diet: many of the mountain tribes regularly hunted r elk, deer, and mountain sheep.

The importance of a mixed hunting, fishing, and gathering economy is flected in this statement by Chief Weninock of the Yakima tribe:

God created the Indian country and it was like he spread out a big blanket. He put the Indians on it. They were created here in this country ... These words are mine and they are true. My strength is from the fish; my blood is from the fish, from the roots and berries. The fish and game are the essence of my life. I was put here by the Creator.

(Chief Weninock, Yakima tribe, 1915)

The Plateau tribes shared in the ideals of a co-operative co-existence, id extensive trade developed between them. Furs and robes were changed by the mountain tribes for products of the seas and rivers from ibes in the valleys who, in turn, maintained contact with coastal groups. ior to the introduction of the horse, transport was primarily by dugout noe and there was regular visiting between members of the numerous llages of semi-subterranean plank- or mat-covered lodges that dotted the ver banks.

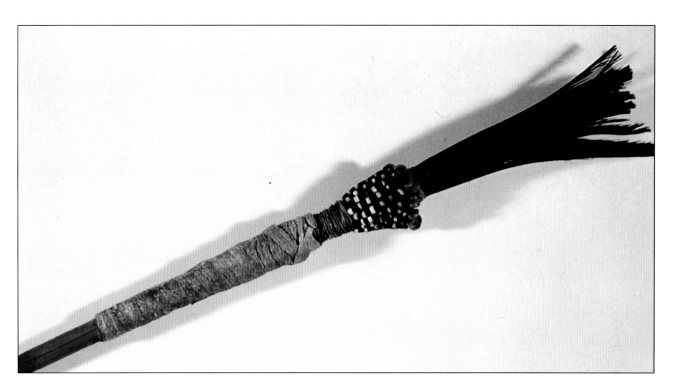

Cayuse

Unlike other Plateau tribes, the Cayuse, living in northeastern Oregon, have gained a reputation for being particularly aggressive and warlike, and it is clear that some specialized weapons were made by them. It is erroneous, however, to believe that this indicates aggressive tendencies in excess of those prevalent in the rest of the area, and the history of their dealings with other tribes suggests that engagement in trading and alliances was far more common.

In fact, Cayuse contacts with the Wallawalla and the Nez Percé were so regular and friendly that many Cayuse families were of mixed blood through inter-marriages. The Cayuse were, however, subject to the missionizing influences of both Catholic and Protestant priests, whose differences of opinion caused resentment and argument. Attempts to establish missions and churches met with refusal because, they said, *'we do not wish to learn to quarrel about God. We may quarrel with men sometimes about things on this earth, but we never quarrel about God.'*

Nevertheless, in 1838, Marcus Whitman, a doctor and self-styled preacher, established a mission among the Cayuse. Although Whitman's

Feather darts, such as this Pomo example, were part of a man's ritual costume in the northern California area, but relate to the 'magic arrows' that shamans were believed capable of sending out to defeat enemies. The example shown here was collected by Captain Vancouver before 1800.

California

The Cayuse of the Plateau gained a reputation for their refusal to accept white arrogance and domination, and consequently became known as an aggressive force in what was, generally, a peaceful and co-operative interaction between the original occupants of the lands and those settlers, farmers, and trappers who came in as outsiders. The Cayuse club shown here was intended as a weapon for use in hand-to-hand fighting and has a white scalp lock attached to it as evidence of its owner's prowess as a warrior.

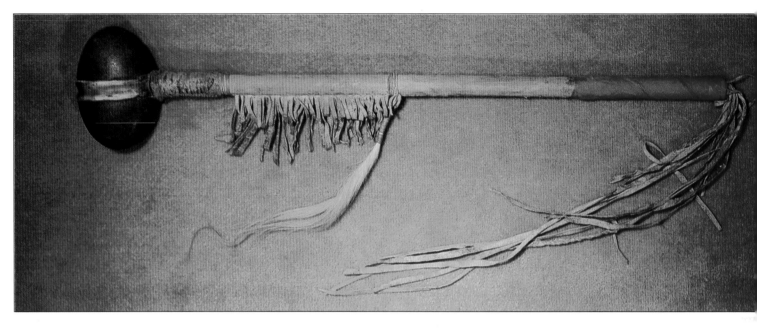

mission does not appear to have been very successful in converting the Cayuse, it remained a troubling presence. Whitman himself was unpopular, due to his adoption of an attitude of arrogant superiority which went contrary to Cayuse ideals and standards of behaviour.

The Cayuse's warlike reputation stems from events of 1847. A smallpox epidemic struck the tribe and when Whitman refused to assist the sick the Cayuse blamed him for the deaths. An argument developed between him and a small group of Cayuse warriors. The angry warriors, seething with resentment at the way Whitman was treating them, descended on the mission during the early hours of the evening and killed Whitman, his wife, and 12 other Americans who worked at the mission.

Local settlers, themselves encroaching on Indian lands, decided to teach the Cayuse a lesson and formed an army. Although the Cayuse managed to avoid a direct confrontation, after a prolonged but indecisive campaign they voluntarily surrendered five members of the tribe who were handed over to the U.S. authorities, charged with the Whitman massacre, and sentenced to death by hanging.

Nez Percé

White intrusions on Indian lands also caused resentment among the Nez Percé, who lived in the Wallowa Valley, 'The Valley of Winding

Waters'. They first came to the attention of the whites in 1805, when the Lewis and Clark expedition left their horses here while they continued by canoe. Lewis and Clark noted the extreme friendliness of the Nez Percé, as well as the fact they had by now largely given up canoe transportation and relied on the horse. Nez Percé contentment and wealth is confirmed in the report of Lewis and Clark that it was not unusual for a single individual to own between 50 and 100 horses.

Problems began with a series of treaties between 1855 and 1877 that attempted to open the Wallowa Valley to white settlement. The Nez Percé led by Heinmot Tooyalaket (Chief Joseph), refused to move, and despite the killing of some Indians by white trespassers, Joseph managed to prevent violence escalating. In explaining his opposition, Chief Joseph made what has become one of the most famous of Indian speeches:

The earth was created by the assistance of the sun, and it should be left as it was ... The country was made without lines of demarcation, and it is no man's business to divide it ... The earth and myself are of one mind. The measure of the earth and the measure of our bodies are the same. Say to us if you can say it, that you were sent by the Creative Power to talk to us. Perhaps you think the Creator sent you here to dispose of us as you see fit. If I thought you were sent by the Creator I might be induced to think you had a right to dispose of me. Do not misunderstand me, but understand me fully with reference to my affection for the land. The one who has the right to dispose of it is the one who has created it. I claim a right to live on my land, and accord you the privilege to live on yours.

(Heinmot Tooyalaket, Nez Percé)

In 1877, however, Chief Joseph's band of Nez Percé agreed to ~~m~~ove; pressures from settlers had increased to the point where it was no ~~lo~~nger tenable for the Nez Percé to remain in their homelands. While ~~pr~~eparing to leave their homes, white settlers ran off with many of the ~~po~~nies in the Nez Percé herds, and a small band of warriors, provoked ~~be~~yond endurance, attacked a white ranch. Joseph, realizing war was ~~in~~evitable, attempted to avoid hostilities by fleeing to Canada. ~~Tr~~avelling fast, though burdened by old men, women, and children, ~~Jo~~seph's little band successfully eluded capture by three separate U.S. ~~fo~~rces through what has been described as the 'most brilliant military ~~str~~ategy'.

Skirmishing with the troops nevertheless took its toll, as did the ~~bit~~ter weather in which the band had been forced to flee. Just 30 miles ~~(5~~0km) from the Canadian border, after travelling over 1,300 miles ~~(2~~,000km) in their desperate flight, General Nelson Miles caught up ~~wi~~th them and blocked their passage. Joseph, seeing that further ~~re~~sistance would lead to unnecessary bloodshed, surrendered to General ~~M~~iles.

I am tired of fighting. Our chiefs are killed. Looking Glass is dead. Toohoolhoolzote is dead. The old men are all dead ... He who led on the young men is dead. It is cold and we have no blankets. The little children are freezing to death. My people, some of them, have run away to the hills, and have no blankets, no food; no one knows where they are – perhaps freezing to death. I want to have time to look for my children and see how many of them I can find. Maybe I shall find them among the dead. Hear me, my chiefs! I am tired; my heart is sick and sad. From where the sun now stands I will fight no more forever.

(Heinmot Tooyalaket, Nez Percé, October 5th, 1877)

~~G~~eneral Miles promised Joseph that the Nez Percé would be returned to ~~th~~eir reservation, but they were instead sent to Indian Territory

(Oklahoma), where many of them sickened and died. By 1885, only 287 captive and dejected Nez Percé remained from what had once been a populous, independent, and proud nation. In his last recorded speech, in 1885, Joseph made an impassioned plea for justice.

General Miles promised that we might return to our own country. I believed General Miles, or I never would have surrendered ... I have heard talk and talk, but nothing is done. Good words do not last long unless they amount to something. Words do not pay for my dead people. They do not pay for my country ... Good words will not give my people good health and stop them from dying. Good words will not get my people a home where they can live in peace and take care of themselves. I am tired of talk that comes to nothing. It makes my heart sick when I remember all the good words and broken promises ... You might as well expect the rivers to run backward as that any man who was born a free man should be contented when penned up and denied liberty to go where he pleases ...

Throughout northern California and into the Northwest Coast area of Washington and British Columbia, iridescent abalone shell was traded as a valuable indicator of family status and wealth. Although abalone can also be gathered off-shore in the northern territories, this is pallid and dull in comparison with that of California. The necklace shown here may have been worn by a prominent Californian woman but, since it was collected by Captain James Cook during his visit to the Northwest Coast, it may be of Californian manufacture but traded to a distinguished family living further north.

The Northwest Coast

OPPOSITE

OPPOSITE
It is impossible to know exactly what spirit-familiar is represented in this Tsimshian or Tlingit mask from the 19th century. That it is a spirit-familiar is, however, clear, since it incorporates elements that depict both human and animal attributes. The entire mask is polished with lead to create a high gloss that would reflect light from the ceremonial fires which blazed when rituals were performed.

In the long ago, when all things were human beings, Whale was the biggest person then as he is the largest animal now. His daughter, Porpoise, had just been admitted into the tsayik dance society, and he was going to give a great feast in her honour. While the guests were waiting for the women to prepare and spread the feast, they had contests of various sorts. Whale appeared carrying a large yew-wood bow which was greater in length than any tree now growing. Its bowstring was twisted whale intestines, and the arrow he carried to be used with the bow was many, many paces in length.

[Whale] said: 'My brothers, this is the great day of my life. My daughter has now done what is necessary to establish her rightful status, except for the feast part of the ceremony which is in preparation. Today I am happy. Now I have a shooting contest for you. To the young man who has strength enough to stretch this bow and shoot this arrow I will give my daughter in marriage.'

Bear was the first to try his skill. He bent his back to lift the log-like bow, but could not raise it a finger's width above the ground. Then he tried to lift just one end of it and even this he could not do. As he retired the lookers-on jeeringly laughed at him.

As Bear sat down, up jumped Cougar. He laughingly remarked, 'Oh, that's nothing. I can shoot that arrow.' But he could not raise the bow a hand's breadth above the ground. Giving up, he declared that no one living, except Whale, could shoot with that bow and arrow and anyone was a fool to try it.

At that moment, up sprang Rabbit. He jumped about the bow and over it several times, chewed on the bowstring for an instant and then

hopped away into the nearby bushes, as everyone laughed loudly. Then, just as the laughing at Rabbit was about to cease, all eyes were turned on Cho-Cho, the Winter Wren. 'Wren,' shouted nearly everyone present, 'try your luck and win the prize. It would do you good to win this young lady. You'd settle down.'

Besides being very handsome, Wren possessed a very violent temper. He threw himself into a passion and began to strut and flutter and hop, as he muttered over and over again his scolding, clamouring, abusive "cho-cho-cho-cho". Then, after he had thus fluttered about for a considerable time, he began to call his tamanawis, guardian spirit power. His tamanawis came to his aid, and soon, small as he was, he went to the great bow and the large arrow. He flew down beside the log-like bow and, to the amazement of all, raised it and put it in position for shooting. Across it he then placed the large-sized arrow. Through the power of his tamanawis, he raised them so that the arrow pointed to the center of the dome of the heavens. For a moment he stood there as he steadied his muscles and took aim. Then the arrow sped forth and out of sight. Down came the bow to the ground with a thud, and Wren fluttered off into the bushes as he uttered his abusive "cho-cho", and at the same time stated he did not wish the prize, for he considered Porpoise too homely to become his wife.

(Adapted from *The War with Heaven*, Quileute Indian)

This story, from the Quileute Indians of the Olympic Peninsula in Washington state, is characteristic of the fabulous tales of mythical beings with enormous powers told by tribes throughout the Northwest Coast. This region, comprising a narrow strip of coastal land stretching

om the Olympic Peninsula, through British Columbia, and into Alaska
far as Yakutat Bay, is a land of mystery and enchantment; a country
which sea mists descend on the land to blot out the horizon and
eate continuity between sea, land, and sky.

The story is typical of the Northwest Coast in a number of features.
ne use of a feast, or potlatch (give-away), to mark the girl's transition
adulthood and reaching marriageable age, the competition between
arious people attending the feast, the use of dramatic dance, the
dicule heaped upon those who fail to meet a challenge, and finally
ren's mocking abuse after he has successfully accomplished a
eemingly impossible task, are all characteristic of Northwest Coast
titudes and beliefs.

Also characteristic is that Wren is able to call on his *tamanawis*, or
irit helpers, to ensure that he succeeds. A belief in the magic powers
one's own personal spirits, in attempts to defeat a rival, is endemic
nong the coastal tribes, and the environment lends power to this belief.
is a brooding, mysterious landscape in which it is easy to understand
e grip that magic and the supernatural can exert in the world of the
ople, as well as where the prodigious forces of nature and the natural
orld are everywhere self-evident.

This sense of grandeur and power is apparent in every aspect of
astal life, from the massive totem poles depicting family lineages that
ere erected outside important houses, to the huge multi-family plank
ouses themselves which are emblazoned with paintings of family
ests. These same crests, depicting the family helpers such as Beaver,
olf, Killerwhale, or Eagle, appear on virtually everything the coastal
dians used. Even such utilitarian objects as fish hooks or ladles are
chly carved and painted.

The spirits appear also in elaborate carved articulated masks, in
hich hidden strings enable, for instance, the beak of Hoxhok, the
annibal Bird, to slam loudly shut; or where a mask depicting Sun
ens radially to reveal Sun's inner power. Such crests, or totems, were
eld in families and passed down through the generations, and the
ossession of them was both jealously guarded and proudly displayed.
he principal venue at which such displays were made was the potlatch,
hen the ancestral powers were celebrated and attempts made to shame
rival family. In the Quileute story the animals are really humans, and
dance impersonations these human-animal qualities are revived
rough the masks and other paraphernalia employed by the dancers.

The Northwest

Northwest Coast plank houses were often painted with elaborate designs depicting family crests. Such designs were indicative of events that supposedly happened in the family's mythological past when an ancestor came into contact with the supernaturals and was given privileges and rights that could then be handed down through the family lineage. The painting on this Kwakiutl house-front depicts a well-known event in which Eagle, shown here with outstretched wings, swoops down to carry off Killerwhale, shown below in skeletal form.

In addition to the ostentatious display of family crests and privileges, the entire area was subject to intense competition. Nowhere else in North America was carving carried to the extremes of the Northwest Coast, but this is intimately connected to the sense of rivalry and competition that the leading families felt for one another. It was through the carvings and masks that status was demonstrated, and the emphasis placed on status accounts for the proliferation of carved images; but at the same time an urgent need was felt to increase the status of one's own family by denigrating that of the other leading families.

Status itself was judged in comparative terms when the family with the greatest number of privileges and the ability to amass the most wealth and host the most lavish feasts and dances gained precedence over their neighbours. Thus the feasts, or potlatches, became a form of 'economic warfare' in which one group attempted to demonstrate that it owned more privileges and more wealth, and could therefore lay claim to more status than another. Because of this, the Northwest Coast tribes claimed to be 'fighting with property'.

A belief in the assistance of ancestral forces and supernatural helpers is nevertheless reflected in the abundance of spirit powers that were thought to occupy the coasts and the narrow belt of temperate rainforest between the coasts and the interior Coastal Mountains. In agreement with the essentially maritime economy of these tribes, since they were primarily fishermen and whalers, the forces of the seas and waters were generally considered more beneficent and helpful than those of the forests.

The forests, in fact, are treacherous and dangerous places. High humidity and an annual rainfall well in excess of 100 inches (2540mm) have turned these into dank, dark, and moss-festooned places, where

This Chugach Eskimo, from an engraving by John Webber who accompanied Captain James Cook's expedition to the Northwest Coast, displays a bewildering array of cross-cultural influences. His hat is reminiscent of those worn by the Nootka of the Queen Charlotte Islands, while lip and nose plugs are of a type usually associated with the Eskimo: his seal-gut parka may have been adopted from either Eskimo or Aleut.

The Northwest

'Button blankets' were indications of a family's rank, clan, and status and were unique to the Northwest Coast. Originally made using small pieces of abalone, they were adapted through European trade when mother-of-pearl buttons became available and began to be used for decoratively outlining the mythological figures with which the blankets were adorned. The Haida example shown here depicts Bear Mother in a characteristic 'open' pose, presenting her hands to the viewer to show that she carries no weapons.

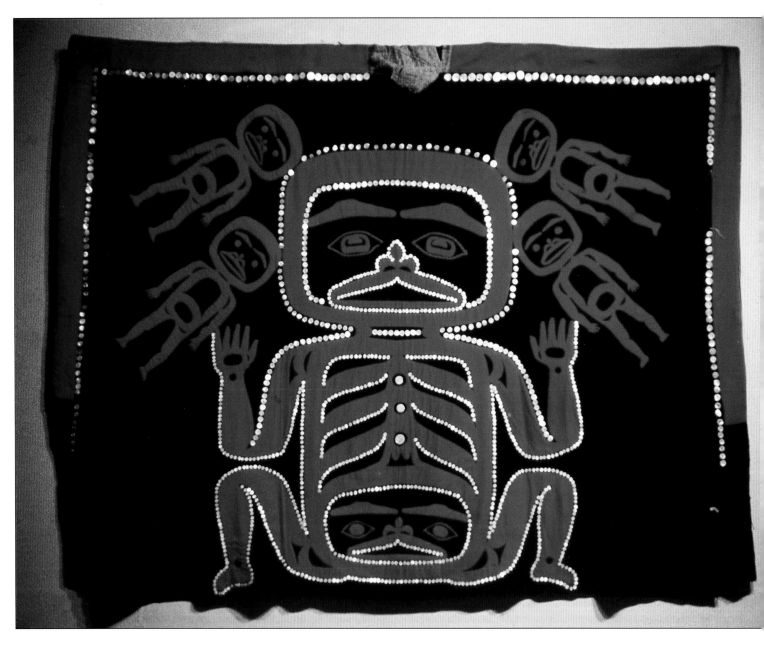

fallen trees lie rotting on the ground beneath lichens that look secure but give way when any weight is put upon them. The forest is the abode of spirits such as Tsonoqua, the Wild Woman of the Woods, whose mournful voice can be heard whistling through the treetops and who will entice the unwary away from their villages to certain death.

The seas, by contrast, provided all the economic necessities for the Northwest Coast tribes, and although the coastal waters, too, could be dangerous – since there are unpredictable eddies and whirlpools in the area – the forces of the sea were more usually friendly and helpful ones, as were the powers of the mammals and fish that occupied them. A positive attitude towards the sea powers is indicated in this shaman's song that attests to the beneficial healing power of the Killerwhale, which is referred to as a life-bringer.

> *Wa haya ha*
> *wa haya ha*
> *I was taken beneath the sea*
> *by the Spirit Power*
>
> *wa haya ha*
> *wa haya ha*
> *dove deep beneath the waves*
> *with the Killerwhale Power*
>
> *wa haya ha*
> *wa haya ha*
> *he took me to his house*
> *called Hole-in-the-Middle-of-the-Sea*
>
> *wa haya ha*
> *wa haya ha*
> *there he threw into me*
> *his healing power*
>
> *wa haya ha*
> *wa haya ha*
> *now I have the life-bringer*
> *the Killerwhale's spirit power*

(Kwakiutl shaman's song to the Killerwhale)

Although the Northwest Coast tribes believed in powerful supernatural helpers and shared a common culture based on wealth, prestige, status, and the use of crests and emblems through which these could be demonstrated, there were nevertheless some clear distinctions between the different groups. Among the northern groups, the Tsimshian, Tlingit, and Haida, there was a particular emphasis on clan affiliation associated with local crests and, among the Haida especially, it was possible for a single clan to occupy an entire village.

The central Kwakiutl and the Nootka did not share this emphasis on clan identity, but instead relied on lineage and blood relationship, this

This Heiltsuk 'welcoming post' from the Kwakiutl tribes of Knight Inlet is carved in the same 'open' posture as the Bear Mother on the button blanket opposite. Figures such as this were erected at the beachheads where villages were located to greet arriving guests and to indicate that a friendly welcome awaited them.

The Northwest

Gambling, sometimes for high stakes, was a common pastime among many Native American groups and was often associated with rituals that had both economic and religious significance. The set of gambling sticks shown below would have been used in a 'hiding game' by the Tlingit, in which the objective was to conceal a marked stick while the opponent attempted to guess where it had been hidden.

being interpreted in the broadest of terms. Thus a person might consider himself related to an entire group even though the actual relationship was only a very vague one. So wide-ranging was this that it was, in fact, possible for a Nootka to consider himself a 'relative' to every other Nootka.

In the south, among the Coast Salish tribes, the direct blood relationship between individuals was the governing factor. The further removed one was from a direct blood tie, the weaker the relationship was considered to be. In many ways this removed some of the intense feuding that took place further north, since rights to inheritance of property and status within the family group were more clearly defined.

There were differences in the arts, too, those of the north being generally more refined and delicate, whereas the central Kwakiutl produced bold polychromatic carvings. Coast Salish carving in the southern regions was, by contrast, relatively limited and relied on simple mass and form rather than the intricate details employed by the

Spielsteine mit Tasche
Tlingit, um 1870. Die 27 Spielstäbe aus Holz sind figürlich geschnitzt. Mischwesen: Bär, Lachs,

Kwakiutl, and placed a greater emphasis on personal guardian spirits than on the family totems that were so common among the tribes further north.

The mainstay of Northwest Coast economies was the salmon, which migrated up-river to spawn in such prodigious numbers that there was little need for any of the tribes to rely on other food sources. Salmon were eaten fresh, smoked, and dried, and special summer 'salmon villages' and house sites were owned by different families and located on the banks of rivers frequented by the fish. So prolific were they that the dried flesh provided ample food throughout the winter as well as sufficient to supply large feasts; thus the entire winter could be spent engaged in ceremonial and ritual pursuits with little need to procure food.

The permanent winter villages consisted of huge gabled houses covered with cedar planking, and were arranged in family groups on beachheads and in sheltered bays, and it was in these that the ceremonies took place. Each house was owned by a family or lineage group, residence generally being patrilocal in the south and matrilocal in the north. Families also owned other resource areas, such as berrying grounds, to which they made exclusive claim.

Coast Salish

The Coast Salish comprise a number of linguistically related groups among whom the extended family was the highest unit of allegiance. So important was the family, that the permanent winter houses usually consisted of a single bloodline, together with women who had married into the group, and each individual was responsible to and for the family. The headman of each household, rather than holding privileges in his own right, was considered to be a trustee of the family privileges, titles and prerogatives.

Such privileges included ownership of ceremonial rights, but extended to cover more practical concerns such as the use of hunting, fishing, and gathering sites. Curiously, since the family was of such primary concern, all these rights and privileges were deemed to stem from the personal contact of an ancestor with a spirit power, when the use of the privilege was granted. Personal spirit contact was also reflected in Spirit Dancing, when an individual who had been in contact with one of the supernatural powers became possessed during

LEFT

This carefully decorated button blanket demonstrates the use of central fields and embroidered borders that were characteristic of central Northwest Coast ceremonial regalia.

remonies and went into trance during which he or she performed a
mimetic dance demonstrating the powers by which he or she was
influenced.

During Coast Salish Winter Ceremonials the Spirit Dancers appear
en masse – since they only return to the people when the cold season
begins – and a ceremonial may involve the participation of several
different tribal groups who are invited from neighbouring areas. There
may be as many as 200 drummers and dancers at a ceremony, each of
them performing as a consequence of a personal revelation which is
demonstrated before a large audience of 'witnesses' who can attest to
the validity of the individual's expression of his or her experience.

Yet although the emphasis is on personal contact with spirit powers,
the family again becomes prominent. Each Spirit Dancer relies on the
intercession of a local shaman, who can interpret the rhythms of the
drum-beat that will encourage the spirit to appear, and it is the shaman
who leads a family group of drummers who repeat this rhythm to induce
trance in the dancer. When several families, villages, and tribes are
represented at a Winter Ceremonial, each of them drums its own
rhythms. The resulting cacophony of sound in these 'dramatizations of
dreams' is said to represent the myriad voices of the spirits.

Unlike the tribes to the north, the Coast Salish had few masked
dances. The Spirit Dancers, although dependent on trance and the
intercession of the spirit power by which they were influenced, did not
attempt to portray the spirits through the use of masks or other ritual
paraphernalia. The spirits' presence was, instead, conveyed by the
movements of the dancers, who danced undulatingly if inspired by sea
creatures, but darted fitfully back and forth if inspired by a power such
as Mosquito.

The only inherited masked dance was that of Xwe-Xwe, a
legendary ancestor who came down from the sky into a lake in Salish
territory and from whom all the Coast Salish are believed to have
descended. Use of this mask was reserved for the use of chiefs' families,
to whom it was an exclusive privilege; but the importance of Xwe-Xwe
can be judged from the fact that the masked dance was also used at
times of personal crisis, when the leading families intervened on behalf
of others. Thus Xwe-Xwe, in addition to its use as a demonstration of
chiefly privileges, might be employed at very personal times in the lives
of other people, such as at marriages and deaths.

The significance of ancestral forces in the lives of the Coast Salish
peoples is apparent in this speech from Chief Seattle, which also
indicates the difference in Salish thinking compared to that of the white
people who attempted to take over Salish lands.

*Yonder sky has wept tears of compassion upon my people for
centuries untold; yet what appears to us as changeless and
eternal may change. Today is fair. Tomorrow may be overcast
with clouds. To us the ashes of our ancestors are sacred and their
resting place is hallowed ground. Our religion is the tradition of
our ancestors – the dreams of our old men, given them in solemn
hours of night by the Great Spirit; and the visions of our sachems*

*The Salish tribes of the Northwest Coast made
large baskets that were used for the storage of
food products. Unlike other tribes of the region
who used naturally occurring dyes to create
patterns, the Salish wove different coloured
vegetable fibres together.*

The Northwest

PAGE 58
With the introduction of steel by Europeans, which provided a more efficient cutting edge than the shell and stone tools previously used, Northwest Coast carving flourished and the smaller carved welcoming posts and house support beams characteristic of an earlier period evolved into majestic cedar totem poles that might be 100 feet (30m) high. The village shown here is that of Skidegate, home to a Haida Indian group on the Queen Charlotte Islands. Unfortunately, well-meaning but misguided missionaries believed such posts were worshipped as 'pagan idols', rather than being representations of the family lineages, and all the poles at Skidegate were cut down in a demonstration of the missionaries' religious zeal.

OPPOSITE
Masked dances were of major importance on the Northwest Coast, when dancers impersonated the mythical supernaturals by which their ancestors had been influenced and which granted rights and privileges to the family lineages. The Kwakiutl bird mask shown here represents one of several celestial beings that were represented during the Dluwulaxa (Those-Who-Descend-From-The-Heavens) dance series.

[medicine men]; and it is written in the hearts of our people. Our dead never forget the beautiful world that gave them being. Day and night cannot dwell together. Tribe follows tribe, and nation follows nation, like the waves of the sea. It is the order of nature, and regret is useless. Every part of this soil is sacred in the estimation of my people. Every hillside, every plain and grove, has been hallowed by some sad or happy event in days long vanished. The very dust upon which you now stand responds lovingly to their footsteps, because it is rich with the blood of our ancestors and our bare feet are conscious of the sympathetic touch. Even the little children who lived here and rejoiced here for a brief season will love these sombre solitudes and at eventide they greet the shadowy returning spirits. The dead are not powerless. Dead, did I say? There is no death, only a change of worlds.

(Chief Seattle, Duwamish Tribe, 1855)

Kwakiutl

Of all the peoples of the Northwest Coast, the central Kwakiutl tribes of Vancouver Island and the adjacent mainland of British Columbia developed the most ostentatious systems of wealth displays and status privileges. These were developed mainly after contact with whites, when the introduction of metal tools made woodworking easier and enabled Kwakiutl carvers to produce work in greater volume.

Central to Kwakiutl belief was the idea that one's lineage was more important than any other consideration, and considerable effort was made to ensure that the 'family' retained a status higher than that of its neighbouring groups. This led to intense competition, and Kwakiutl potlatches became known for their excess.

Challenges to a rival family might be issued a year or more in advance of the competition potlatch, and during the period leading up to the event the lineage manufactured and collected masses of goods that would be given away in displays of their wealth. The more that could be distributed by way of bigger feasts, and the greater the boasts of the host group, the higher the status that could be claimed. So excessive was this that the Kwakiutl during the 19th century were unable to manufacture sufficient quantities of goods to fuel the potlatches, and instead had to invent a system of marked tally sticks which represented predetermined values.

Thus a stick marked with ten lines might represent a value of 100 Hudson Bay blankets – the Hudson's Bay blanket having become a standardized measure of value following its introduction through trade.

The principle behind the potlatch was, quite simply, to bankrupt one's neighbours. A rival lineage could not refuse to attend a potlatch for fear of losing face and being held to ridicule, but once an invitation had been accepted they were placed in a position where they had to accept the goods on offer. Having accepted these, they were then obliged to hold a return potlatch at which the goods would be returned but at 100 per cent interest. It was only by doing this that they could demonstrate that their own lineage was capable of hosting potlatches of even greater magnitude, and could thereby claim higher status and prestige.

That the Kwakiutl themselves considered this a form of 'economic warfare' is clear from numerous speeches which have been recorded and in which the rival is referred to in derogatory terms. They also make specific reference to the fact that they are 'fighting with wealth'.

Friends, I ask you to keep yourselves in readiness, for the Koskimo are like to a vast mountain of wealth, from which rocks are rolling down all the time. If we do not defend ourselves, we shall be buried by their property. Behold, friends! They are dancing and making merry day after day. But we are not doing so. Remember, this is our village and our battlefield. If we do not open our eyes and awake, we shall lose our high rank. Remember, we have never been vanquished by another tribe.

(Potlatch speech given at Fort Rupert, 1895)

Although the principle of potlatching, essentially of gift-giving and feasting, was prevalent in Kwakiutl society and used on every occasion when a change of status occurred, such as the coming-of-age of a daughter, it was most marked during the Winter Ceremonials of the Kwakiutl Secret Societies – particularly those of the Dluwulaxa (Those-Who-Descend-From-The-Heavens) and of the Hamatsa (Cannibals), at which the high-ranking sons and daughters of the principal families inherited rights from their elders.

The inheritance of such privileges, which included the right to wear certain masks and to sing the associated songs, to perform particular dances, use privileged names, and so forth, was the occasion for extremely lavish gift-giving. At times, however, a disregard for wealth was exhibited by destroying valuable property. Dugout canoes,

elaborately painted and sometimes 50 feet (15m) or more in length, might be broken to pieces, or eulachon oil – a valuable commodity since it could only be obtained through trade with the northern tribes – might be burned. At other times the oil might be wasted in a 'grease feast', when the rival 'chief' was challenged to consume as much as possible; the chief, however, as representative of the lineage, might delegate the actual consumption to a team of family members.

In the course of such conspicuous consumption, the challenged chief would mock his rival by stating how miserly he was in providing so little, even though the quantities were in fact enormous; or would sit close to the fire in which grease was being burned, claiming that his host was too niggardly to provide enough heat to keep him warm. Legend has it that one chief, mocked by his rival for burning so little eulachon oil, poured such quantities of it onto the fire that the flames leaped as high as the roof of the building and threatened to burn it down. Meanwhile, his opponent sat unmoving close to the fire, despite the fact that the heat was so intense that his skin began to blister.

During this ordeal the challenged chief displayed his scorn thus: *I thought another one was causing the smoky weather? I am the only one on earth – the only one in the world – who makes thick smoke rise from the beginning of the year to the end, for the invited tribes. What will my rival say again – that 'spider woman'; what will he pretend to do next? The words of that 'spider woman' do not go a straight way. Will he not brag that he is going to give away canoes, that he is going to break coppers, that he is going to give a grease feast? Such will be the words of the 'spider woman' and therefore your face is dry and mouldy* [that is, he appears as if he were a ghost]*, you who are standing in front of the stomachs of the chiefs.*

(Potlatch reply song, sung to ridicule one's host)

The reference to 'smoky weather' is to the thick black smoke caused by burning eulachon oil at the grease feast, whereas that to 'coppers' refers to the shield-shaped plaques of Native copper that were so rare they had values expressed in terms of thousands of Hudson's Bay blankets. Coppers were only significant in the context of the potlatch, and each time one was used its value doubled; thus a copper worth, say, 5,000 blankets and given to a rival would be worth 10,000 when potlatched to another rival at a later date. By 'breaking' a copper,

that is, by cutting it into pieces and throwing it away instead of giving it to a rival, no return was expected; although the rival was then under an obligation to break and destroy another copper or property worth double its value to remain 'even'.

Both the Dluwulaxa and the Hamatsa Societies were essentially dramatizations of ancestral supernatural experiences, at which the principal dancers wore masks and re-enacted the ancestral contact through which gifts were given by a spirit. Such gifts then became the hereditary property of the lineage. The Society dances are often referred to as Winter Ceremonials since winter was *tsetseka*, or sacred; the time of year when economic activities were suspended and the important houses ritually cleansed and purified for the ceremonies soon to take place.

Both the Dluwulaxa and the Hamatsa dances served to initiate important sons and daughters, during which the dance paraphernalia was handed down from a parent and the event was witnessed and solemnized by invited guests, usually in the form of a potlatch for a rival. The main difference between the two dance series was in the type of ancestral contact that was demonstrated. In the Hamatsa dances an emphasis was placed on encounters with the monsters which menace the spectators and destroy property. The dances were marked by theatrical tricks and illusions, often of a macabre or violent nature.

The Dluwulaxa, by contrast, featured supernatural beings such as Star, Cloud, and Bird, as well as spirits of the seas, and did not include the violent and destructive features of the Hamatsa dances. Dluwulaxa dances were orderly and sedate, but no less dramatic than those of the Hamatsa. Some of the masks were elaborate compositions, often articulated through the use of hidden strings. These represented the magical powers of the supernatural beings and were used in association with songs that were also considered to have magical properties. It was through these songs that the 'novice' who was inheriting the masks and privileges was 'called down' from the skies to take part in the performance.

Nootka

The Nootka of western Vancouver Island and Nootka Sound shared many of the customs of the Kwakiutl, including the belief that supernaturals descended from the skies to bestow blessings and the use of the potlatch to validate inherited rights and privileges. They did not, however, go to the extremes of the Kwakiutl and the potlatch was not intended to mock a rival. Return gifts were expected, but there was no compulsion to repay these with interest or even to match those that had previously been given away. There was no property destruction and no use of coppers.

Potlatches were held principally during the main Nootka ceremony known as Nutlam, or Wolves, in which the initiates – usually children who had reached the age of puberty – were captured by dancers representing the Wolves and taken away for secret instruction referring to the origin of some hereditary right. Much of the Nutlam, however, was a farce in which comic acts played an important part as 'wolf experts', using any number of ludicrous and ingenious traps, attempted to catch the Wolves and rescue the kidnapped children.

Like the Dluwulaxa and Hamatsa dances of the Kwakiutl, the Nutlam served to define an individual's place in the social order through the inheritance of different names and crests. Those of the highest rank, who had several names and crests, might in fact be initiates at several different performances to enable them to be instructed in the various dances and songs that accompanied each of the inherited privileges. Everyone, however, performed at least once, on the occasion of acquiring an adult name that was held as 'property' within the family lineage.

In addition to the ownership of names, crests, and dances, certain professions, such as whaling, carving, and so on, were also inherited privileges, as was that of being a trader. The Nootka were in fact well known as traders, and often bartered the dugout canoes they made to other coastal tribes; but they were especially famed for their prowess in hunting the larger sea creatures. One of the most important privileges, reserved only for chiefly lines, was that of the whale hunter, since only a chief had the right to wield a harpoon. Whale hunting was accompanied by a great deal of ritual and ceremony, much of which was in the form of incantations or prayers intended to appease the whale and to encourage it to approach the whaling boats.

LEFT

Beaver, depicted here on a pole which is possibly of Bella Coola origin, was a powerful supernatural helper. Poles such as this were erected in front of family dwellings to indicate the clan association of the occupants and to describe events that had occurred during the family's ancestral past.

The Northwest

OPPOSITE ABOVE

In order to validate their rights to possess and express prestigious status and social prominence, wealthy families on the Northwest Coast had to finance elaborate feasts, or potlatches, at which excessive quantities of goods were distributed to invited guests. This Tlingit basketry hat is surmounted by a number of cedar-bark rings, each indicating a successful potlatch hosted by its owner.

OPPOSITE BELOW

Tsonoqua, the Wild-Woman-of-the Woods, was a powerful figure whose voice could be heard whistling through the treetops. She is shown here in this Kwakiutl carving from Cape Mudge with a characteristic pursed mouth through which her vocalizations were projected.

RIGHT

Although all the peoples of the Northwest Coast were renowned for their abilities as maritime hunters and fishers, the Nootka achieved a reputation as expert whalers. This hat, depicting a whaling scene, would have been worn by a prominent Nootkan chief during the rites preceding a whale hunt. Whaling among the Nootka was considered a prestigious activity and only chiefs and their sons had the right to wield whaling harpoons.

Whale, I want you to come near me, so that I will get hold of your heart and deceive it, so that I will have strong legs and not be trembling and excited when the whale comes and I spear him.
Whale, you must not run out to sea when I spear you.
Whale, if I spear you, I want my spear to strike your heart.
Harpoon, when I use you, I want you to go to the heart of the whale.
Whale, when I spear at you and miss you, I want you to take hold of my spear with your hands.
Whale, do not break my canoe, for I am going to do good to you.
I am going to put eagle-down and cedar-bark on your back [that is, the whale will be ceremonially blessed when brought ashore]
Whale, if I use only one canoe to kill you, I want to kill you dead.

(Nootkan prayer of the whaler)

Haida and Tlingit

The Haida, living on the Queen Charlotte Islands, and the Tlingit of the northern British Columbian and southern Alaskan coasts, share similar beliefs to the other Northwest Coast tribes, but place a stronger emphasis on the use of shamanic powers and in the important social standing enjoyed by a shaman.

Among the Haida, in particular, the village leader or headman was often a shaman rather than a chief, and the shaman's status was not infrequently ranked higher than that of any other member of the community; whereas the Tlingit felt that shamans were in a special class of their own, their status belonging to the realms of the supernatural and equal to that of the chiefs in the secular world. The importance of the shamans among both the Haida and Tlingit is indicated by the fact that war could only be declared by a shaman and the training of warriors, as well as leadership of the war party, was entrusted to a shaman.

The emphasis placed on the shamans' role was linked to their ability to foretell the future and to influence future events. In times of warfare, the shaman guided the war party by lying face down in the prow of the canoe so that his spirits could predict where the enemy were to be found. It is said that the shaman sent his spirits to search for the enemy villages or canoes and they reported back to him and told him which direction to take.

As with the secret societies, the spirits that inspired the shamans gave them names, songs, dances, and stories which were limited to the claimants of shamanic power. These, however, were not generally inherited rights. Instead, the potential shaman 'saw' a vision or had an omen which guided him and granted the right to practise, but training was usually given by an established shaman whom the initiate's family paid for this service.

It is nevertheless clear that becoming a shaman – although theoretically vision-inspired – was an efficient means whereby a person from a relatively low-status family could acquire wealth and a position of social importance. Most shamans were, or became, wealthy through their practice, since they could demand high fees for their services. Indeed, it was often felt that the more a shaman was paid to conduct a cure the more effort would be expended on the shaman's part. As most illnesses were thought to be caused by a sorcerer or a rival shaman, it was apparent that cures – which were made by removing an imaginary 'disease-causing' object – could only be effected with the assistance of the shaman's supernatural helpers.

Shamans acquired wealth through other activities. As the leaders of war parties they might be entitled to captured crests and privileges from a rival group, but they were also paid to assist in numerous other affairs, including the making of marriage proposals on behalf of members of the clan, ensuring success in hunting and fishing, controlling the weather, manufacturing love charms and potions, and supervising old women acting as midwives during childbirth. There were few aspects of life that did not demand shamanic intercession or guidance and, where healing was concerned, it was generally felt that the more one paid the more effort would be put into ensuring its efficacy.

Tsimshian

Located on the Nass and Skeena Rivers in British Columbia, the Tsimshian tribes shared in the general cultural ethos of the Northwest Coast except that their location enabled them to rely heavily on trading as a principal part of their economy, since they occupied the only direct river access to the interior along most of the coast. The copper used by tribes such as the Kwakiutl was traded into the area by the Tsimshian from tribes living in the north; slaves captured from the Salish were traded to northern groups, otter skins were traded from the Haida, and dentalium shells – important in the decoration of ritual costumes and artefacts – were brought by them to other tribes from a variety of sources.

The mainstay of Tsimshian trade, however, was eulachon oil. The eulachon, or candle-fish, makes an annual spring run which precedes that of the salmon, and the heaviest occurs at Red Bluffs on the lower Nass River in Tsimshian-held territory. Whole canoe-loads of eulachon were thrown into pits to partially decompose and then put into wooden boxes which were filled with water. By dropping red-hot stones into the mixture it quickly came to the boil, and the rich oil floated to the surface from where it was scooped out and allowed to cool and thicken.

Even when the Hudson's Bay Company established a trading post called Fort Simpson at Metlakatla Pass, the Tsimshian quickly appropriated some of the trade for themselves by acting as middlemen. Hudson's Bay goods, particularly the blankets that were unbiquitous among the coast tribes, were obtained in trade by the Tsimshian and then bartered to other tribes at a profit.

Tsimshian contact with other groups through trade is also reflected in their ceremonialism and secret societies which are clearly borrowed. Their major dancing societies were those of the Nutlam, borrowed from the Nootka, and of the Dluwulaxa, obtained from the Kwakiutl. Even some of the spirits were known by their Kwakiutl names and the songs associated with them sung in Kwakiutl. The wide-ranging contacts made by the Tsimshian are shown in this shamanic song:

I go in my canoe
all over
in my vision.
Over trees
or in water
I'm floating.
All around
I float
among whirlpools.
All around
I float
among shadows.
I go in my canoe
all over
in my vision.
Over trees
or in water
I'm floating.
Whose canoe is this
I stand in.
The one
I stand in
with a stranger.
I go in my canoe
all over
in my vision.
Over trees
or in water
I'm floating.

(Vision song of Isaac Tens, Tsimshian shaman)

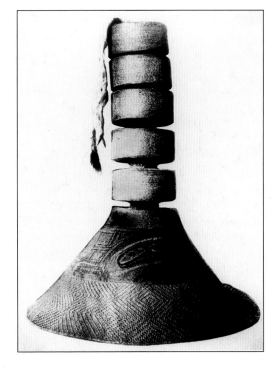

The Plains and Prairies

The buffalo, or bison, was the mainstay of the economy of Plains tribes, and provided virtually every necessity of life: from food, clothing, and shelter, to fuel, glue, and cordage. After the European re-introduction of the horse in the 1700s (native horses having become extinct at the close of the Pleistocene Ice Age), hunting on horseback became the favoured method. The painting shown opposite is after an illustration of the 1830s by Carl Bodmer, who accompanied Prince Maximilian zu Wied during his explorations of the Upper Missouri.

The grasslands of the Plains and Prairies in the interior of the North American continent were home to what has come to be regarded as the archetypal Native American. It is here that we find feathered war bonnets, scalp-decorated war shirts, the use of the horse, a dependency on buffalo hunting, and, in short, all the attributes of the 'Hollywood' Indian that are so familiar through tales of the Wild West and Cowboy and Indian movies.

The popular myth is nevertheless exploded when we consider Plains and Prairie culture in greater detail. Chief Luther Standing Bear said:

We did not think of the great open plains, the beautiful rolling hills, and winding streams with tangled growth, as 'wild'. Only to the white man was nature a 'wilderness' and only to him was the land 'infested' with 'wild' animals and 'savage' people. To us it was tame. Earth was bountiful and we were surrounded with the blessings of the Great Mystery. Not until the hairy man from the east came and with brutal frenzy heaped injustices upon us and the families we loved was it 'wild' for us. When the very animals of the forest began fleeing from his approach, then it was for us that the 'Wild West' began. (Chief Luther Standing Bear, Oglala Sioux)

The Plains and Prairies encompass the area from the Rocky Mountains to the Mississippi Valley and from Texas and Oklahoma north into Canada. The entire area is grassland, with shorter 'buffalo grass' in the west and more luxuriant taller grasses in the eastern regions, and is marked by cold winters and hot summers. The area once supported a remarkable number of animals, particularly the prong-horn antelope and buffalo which originally numbered many millions. This led to an essentially hunting culture, although the Prairie tribes of the east also practised agriculture, growing maize, beans, squash, and pumpkins.

Regarded as stereotypical of the Native American way of life, Plains culture was nevertheless a very recent phenomenon which was only able to develop fully after the introduction of the horse and the gun by Europeans in the 18th century. Prior to that, the grasslands had been occupied by only a few small family groups of pedestrian nomads with little tribal cohesion who lived in much the same way as the prehistoric hunters and gatherers had done since the end of the Ice Age. Such early gatherers numbered only a few individuals and were forced into a nomadic existence as they followed the animal migrations and the seasonal ripening of berries and wild roots.

The horse and the gun, however, were to revolutionize the lives of these people, and also enticed many other groups into the grasslands area. The characteristics of Plains life, which includes a warrior ethos in which courage was lauded, the development of systems of democratic leadership, warrior societies, raiding, and the buffalo chase, all came about as a result of the horse and gun. But it was the buffalo more than anything else that determined the life of the Plains Indians. One of the friars travelling with Coronado, who met the southern Plains tribes, wrote of the Indian's dependence on the buffalo.

With the skins they make their houses, with the skins they clothe and shoe themselves, of the skins they make rope, and also of the wool; from the sinews they make thread, with which they sew their clothes and also their houses; from the bones they make awls; the dung serves them for wood, because there is nothing

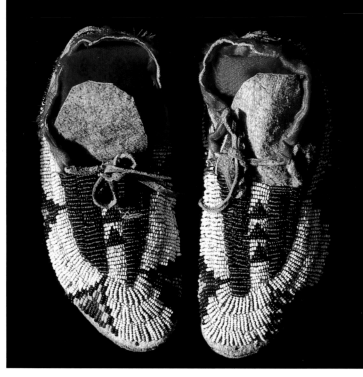

ABOVE, LEFT and RIGHT
Plains tribes formerly decorated items of
costume with dyed porcupine quills, but quickly
adopted beads when these became available
through trade with Europeans. The moccasins
shown here bear beaded patterns that are
characteristic of northern Plains tribes.

OPPOSITE ABOVE
Plains beaded moccasins, probably Kiowan. The
Indian aesthetic extended to every aspect of their
lives and great care was taken to ensure that
even simple everyday items of apparel, such as
these moccasins, expressed their sense of
harmony with the world about them.

else in that country; the stomachs serve them as pitchers and
vessels from which they drink; they live on the flesh.

After the coming of the white man the horse was adopted and led to a dramatic change in the lives of the Plains Indians. The horse made the pursuit of buffalo easy and was perfectly suited to a grassland environment. It also encouraged raiding, since the acquisition of horses became an ideal to which young warriors aspired as well as a symbol of wealth. Greater mobility (for the tribes had previously relied on the dog as their only means of transporting their buffalo-hide tipis and other goods) led to an intensification of the nomadic habit. Tribes were able to carry larger quantities of goods and cover greater distances than they ever had in the past.

Yet despite the emphasis on a warrior ethos and the encouragement of young men to embark on deeds of daring and courage, there was little reference to killing enemies in Plains tradition. It was, in fact, felt more courageous to ride up to an armed enemy and strike him without causing harm, and then to ride away, than it was to ambush him from the safety

of shelter. Striking an armed enemy who could fight back counted far higher on the 'coup' system (from the French for a blow), since it entailed greater danger than the taking of a scalp from a dead person unable to strike back.

It was nevertheless clear that high status pivoted on the accumulation of a successful war record, which was generally reckoned in terms of the number of enemy horses an individual had managed to capture. The highly trained buffalo ponies, which were used exclusively for buffalo hunting and usually tethered close to their owner's tipis, were highly prized, since to capture one meant entering the heart of the enemy camp to cut the pony loose.

Yet the acquisition of wealth was clearly motivated by other factors, since material goods constituted a hindrance in the nomadic life of the Plains Indians. Tribes moved regularly and the more goods an individual possessed the more difficult it was to travel around. Many of the captured horses were given away to poorer members of the tribe or were recaptured in enemy raids, and the massive herds owned by individuals

LEFT
*At certain times of the year when the small
nomadic bands of Plains Indians gathered for
tribal ceremonies and communal hunts, the
people were given to public displays that
frequently involved parades and demonstrations
of horsemanship. At such times, horses were
elaborately decorated with beaded and quilled
ornaments such as this Crow rosette.*

n the Plateau – where a single person might own 100 horses or more –
were unknown on the Plains.

Also important in Plains and Prairie reckoning of an individual's
worth were the qualities of virtuousness and generosity – so much so
that the chiefs, who had often given away virtually all their property to
the less able members of the community, frequently possessed fewer
material goods than others. To gain prominent status in these societies it
was necessary to display bravery and generosity, but also to demonstrate
a willingness to adhere to strict standards of truth, honesty, self-control,
courtesy, respect for superiors, industry, and thrift.

Although Plains culture was similar throughout this vast region, the
tribes can nevertheless be divided into characteristic groups. There were
those of the northern Plains, the Blackfoot, Plains Cree, Plains Ojibwa,
Gros Ventre, and Sarsi; tribes of the central region, including the Sioux,
and Crow; those of the south, the Comanche, Kiowa, and Kiowa-
Apache; and the semi-nomadic tribes of the Mississippi-Missouri,
among whom are the Mandan, Hidatsa, Pawnee, Osage, and Omaha.

The Plains and Prairies

RIGHT

Powder Face, an Arapaho warrior, is shown here wearing a long feathered war bonnet to demonstrate the martial achievements of his warrior society and carries a decorated staff which is indicative of his society membership.

FAR RIGHT

All Plains tribes made particular efforts to display family prestige and status through elaborate decoration of costumes worn on public occasions. The Sioux woman shown here has the yoke of her dress richly embellished with elk teeth, and also wears a necklace made from tubular shells that indicate trade contacts.

Plains tribes took a great deal of pride in their families, and children were frequently indulged and given many signs of recognition and affection. The two Kiowa girls shown here are wearing highly-decorated dresses indicative of their family's prominent status. Note in particular the dress of the younger girl, which is decorated with elk teeth. Since only two teeth from the elk were used and the Kiowa had to travel and trade extensively with the northern tribes to obtain them, such a dress was considered very valuable.

The Plains and Prairies

RIGHT

Sitting Bull, a Sioux shaman, was one of the outstanding leaders in the Plains tribes' fight to prevent white settlers taking over their lands. Adamantly opposed to white dominance, he led his small band of Hunkpapa families into brief refuge in Canada before returning to captivity on the Pine Ridge Reservation where he was brutally murdered on 15 December 1890.

OPPOSITE LEFT

Keokuk, shown in this daguerreotype of 1847, was a war leader of the Sauk who bitterly opposed British colonial efforts to subjugate the tribes of the Woodlands and Plains. Despite his opposition to the British he was nevertheless a man of peace and sought, wherever possible, to resolve difficulties by diplomatic means. He is shown here wearing a James Monroe peace medal, awarded to him for his untiring efforts to reach an amicable settlement.

OPPOSITE RIGHT

Quanah Parker, of the Kwahadi band of the Comanche of the southern Plains, came to prominence in the 1870s when, at only 27 years old, he became the tribes's undisputed war leader. Son of a Kwahadi chief and a captive white woman, Elizabeth Parker, Quanah was nevertheless an implacable foe of the whites and was the last Comanche chief to surrender.

Blackfoot

The Algonquian-speaking Blackfoot, living in Montana and Alberta, were the dominant tribe of the northern Plains. Blackfoot tradition says they came from the east, and their language – though much changed – appears to be related to that of the tribes living in the vicinity of the Great Lakes. By the time contact was first made, the Blackfoot were nevertheless fully integrated into the Plains way of life.

The Blackfoot were not a single tribe but a confederacy of the Siksika (Northern Blackfoot, or Blackfoot Proper), the Piegan (with Northern and Southern divisions), and the Kainah (or Blood), together with their allies, the Athapascan-speaking Sarsi. Between 1750 and 1770, the Blackfoot, having acquired horses and guns through trade, began to expand their hunting and raiding territories, and as a result made enemies of virtually every tribe with whom they came in contact.

The Blackfoot explain the origin of war in the tale of Scar-Face, a young man who wished to marry the beautiful daughter of the chief, but was told that unless he removed the ugly scar that marked his face he would be refused. In a search for supernatural assistance, Scar-Face travelled to the home of Sun, where he killed seven vicious Cranes that threatened the life of Sun's son, Morning Star. He cut off the Cranes' heads as proof of his heroic deed and thus originated the practice of decapitating or scalping a killed enemy. Sun, in gratitude, removed the scar and gave him black-striped leggings which he was to wear as a demonstration of his warrior status, and which Blackfoot warriors wore ever after in celebratory dances.

Yet although they were a dominant force who effectively prevented white trappers and hunters from seizing their territories, and whom they raided for their furs which they then sold to the Hudson's Bay Company, the Blackfoot never engaged in any major wars with the white man. The only serious conflict occurred in the winter of 1869-1870 when U.S. troops under the command of Major Eugene Baker attacked a peaceful southern Piegan village led by Heavy Runner. Of the 219 Indians in the camp, mostly old men, women, and children, only 46 survived: 33 men, 90 women, and 50 children were slaughtered.

In earlier days the Blackfoot could, and would, have reacted in force against such brutality; but by the time this massacre occurred, their numbers had been vastly reduced by smallpox, which struck their camps in 1836, 1845, 1857, and again in 1870, reducing the population by more than two-thirds. With the extermination of the buffalo herds in the 1880s, the Blackfoot were compelled to sign treaties and to remove to reservations which, though located on their original lands, represented only a fraction of the country they had previously controlled.

Their most famous chief, Crowfoot, renowned for his ability as a diplomat and orator and famed for preserving the peace and preventing Blackfoot warriors joining with the Sioux under the leadership of Sitting Bull in their wars with the Whites, commented in 1890, shortly before his death that same year, on the fleeting nature of existence:

What is life? It is the flash of a firefly in the night. It is the breath of a buffalo in the winter time. It is the little shadow which runs across the grass and loses itself in the sunset.

(Crowfoot, Blackfoot chief, April 1890)

Sioux

he Siouan-speaking tribes of the Dakotas are perhaps the best known of
e Native American groups, due primarily to their resistance to white
vasions of their lands and their desperate struggle against U. S. forces
nder the leadership of such prominent men as Sitting Bull and Crazy
orse. Wamditanka explained why the Sioux resisted the incursions of
e whites so vehemently:

*The whites were always trying to make the Indians give up their
life and live like white men – go to farming and do as they did –
and the Indians did not know how to do that, and did not want to
anyway ... If the Indians had tried to make the whites live like
them, the whites would have resisted, and it was the same way
with us.*

(Wamditanka, or Big Eagle, Santee Sioux)

Tatanka Yotanka, Sitting Bull, expressed a similar idea the year after
s and Crazy Horse's Sioux, together with their Cheyenne allies, had
efeated General George Armstrong Custer's troops at the Battle of the
ittle Bighorn, when he said that his objection to the Americans was:

*Because I am a red man. If the Great Spirit had desired me to be
a white man he would have made me so in the first place. He put
in your hearts certain wishes and plans, in my heart he put other
and different desires. Each man is good in his sight. It is not
necessary for eagles to be crows. Now we are poor but we are
free. No white man controls our footsteps. If we must die we die
defending our rights.*

(Tatanka Yotanka, or Sitting Bull, Hunkpapa Sioux chief, 1877)

The spirit of warfare that led leaders such as Sitting Bull and
razy Horse to passionately defend the rights of their people was
eeply ingrained in the Sioux psyche. Young men were brought up on
e adage that it was 'better to die young in battle than to grow old and
elpless' and a familiar war cry was 'Hoka hey! Follow me! Today is a
ood day to fight, today is a good day to die.' Bravery and courage, as
mong other Plains tribes, were the outstanding characteristics of Sioux
arriors. Yet it would be incorrect to assume that Siouan warriors lived
nly for war or that warfare with American forces over the occupation of
ndian lands and the senseless slaughter of the buffalo by white hunters
as typical of the aboriginal pattern.

Aboriginally, war was played almost as a 'game' which,

although a dangerous one, was carried out according to strict codes of
honour. Weaker tribes not invariably found protection from stronger
groups, since courage was best expressed by challenging those who were
in a position to retaliate and fight back. It is also characteristic of hunting
tribes, where long periods of inactivity waiting for game were followed
by short, sudden, and explosive periods of violent activity. This hunting
ethos was carried over into Siouan relations with neighbouring tribal
groups.

Warfare was, nevertheless, governed by a deep love of life and of the
spiritual forces that protected each individual. Every Sioux warrior went
on a vision quest during which he fasted and prayed in some lonely and
isolated spot for the supernaturals to grant him their blessing and provide
some positive sign of their protective power. This usually came through
the intercession of an animal or bird that gave the vision-seeker face- and
body-paints, and a song, that could be used before going into battle to
provide protection and guidance.

Such spirit forces were thought to abound in every aspect of the
natural world, and it was with deep reverence that the Sioux viewed the
lands they occupied: this, of course, was part of the reason for their
clashes with the Americans, whom they considered to be defiling the
land by showing disrespect for the forces it contained. But a similar
respect for nature and natural powers was displayed by the other tribes
with whom they came into conflict and Indian battles were often
postponed while each side appealed to the powers that protected the
warriors. Tatanka Ohitika, commenting on the forces that controlled
nature, said:

*When I was ten years of age I looked at the land and the rivers,
the sky above, and the animals around me and could not fail to
realize that they were made by some great power.*

(Tatanka Ohitika, or Brave Buffalo, Sioux shaman, 1911)

Even Sitting Bull ascribed his survival – in an encounter with a
grizzly bear when he was a young man, and when he survived by
pretending to be dead – to the intercession of the spirit powers who
appeared to him in the form of a small bird, the yellow-hammer:

*Pretty Bird, you saw me and took pity on me;
You wished me to survive among the people.
O Bird People, from this day always you shall be my relatives!*

OPPOSITE

*Traditionally, Plains tipis were made from
buffalo hides, as can be seen in the irregular
patterning and heavy seams in this photograph of
an Arapaho camp made about 1870. Shortly
after this date, with the demise of the buffalo
caused by white hunters and 'sportsmen' and the
introduction of a reservation system with its
associated trade goods and annuities, all tipis
were manufactured from canvas.*

LEFT

Although many Plains warriors rode naked into battle, it was usual for them to carry some form of 'medicine' which would afford them protection. At times, the medicine might be incorporated into costume items such as this Blackfoot 'perforated' shirt which was said to provide protection by enabling bullets and arrows to pass through the holes, avoiding injury to the wearer.

BELOW

Right: On ceremonial and other public occasions, Plains women wore richly-decorated dresses that indicated not only their family status but also the women's individual skills as beadworkers. The beaded yoke on this Sioux dress is a splended example of such decorative skills.

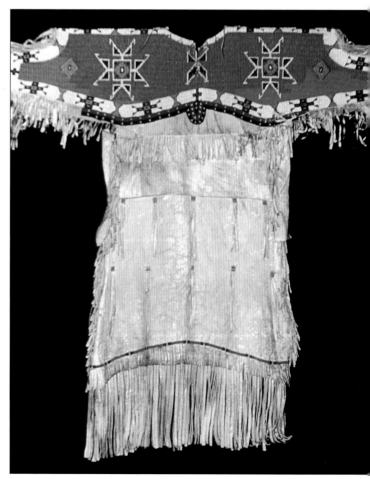

Crow

Although only a small tribe, the Crow, living in the basins of the Yellowstone and Bighorn Rivers in Montana, occupied the richest hunting grounds in the Plains and vigorously defended these against incursions by other tribal groups, including the Blackfoot and Sioux. Described as 'the most handsome of Plains tribes, and with the most elegant tipis', they also possessed the largest herds of horses. With a population that probably never exceeded 4,000, the Crow in the early historic period were estimated to own as many as 10,000 horses. Although this number is small in comparison with the herds of the Nez Percé of the Plateau, with whom the Crow traded extensively, it was nevertheless vast in comparison with other Plains tribes where the average numbers of horses per person rarely exceeded one.

Because of the richness of the land and their wealth in horses the Crow inevitably became the target for raiding by other groups. They were in conflict with the Blackfoot, Sarsi, and Gros Ventre alliance to their north; with the Siouan tribes to the east; with the Cheyenne on their southern borders; and with the Flathead tribes to their west. For the Crow, the necessity for warfare and accumulation of war honours is reflected in the fact that to become a chief or distinguished warrior it was necessary for a man to count four coups which were striking first coup on an uninjured enemy, taking a bow or gun in a hand-to-hand encounter, taking a picketed horse from outside its owner's lodge, and leading a successful war-party.

Unlike many Plains tribes, who had migrated into the region from beyond the borders of the Plains, the Crow separated from the semi-nomadic and partly agricultural Hidatsa living on the Upper Missouri. As a result, they retained some farming traditions, particularly the planting of sacred tobacco. This is shown in the importance of the Tobacco Society among the Crow, when benefits and prestige accrued to members since it was believed their activities brought blessings to the tribe as a whole.

A warrior tradition was nevertheless introduced even into the Tobacco Society. Two warriors, one to cook the consecrated buffalo tongues that were a required part of the ritual and the other to fetch water, which was done as if reporting the successful return of a war-party, were essential to the initiation of a new member. They both had to be able to recite coups they had achieved and to have the right to sing 'praise songs' which celebrated their victories over a defeated enemy.

Although steeped in the traditions of warfare so common among Plains tribes, Crow narratives reflect their attitude that things should never be taken too seriously. When stories were being recited it was expected that the audience should mutter 'e, e, e' at regular intervals to show they had not fallen asleep, and if they failed to do so the story-teller would simply abandon his attempt to relate the tale. Many of these stories poked fun at other tribal members, and verbal dexterity was highly esteemed.

Perhaps the most distinctive element in Crow narratives was the use of punning and of tongue-twisters which were intended to be repeated quickly and accurately. The best-known of these is *basakapupe'cdec*

As the mainstay of Plains economies the buffalo was accorded status and respect that elevated it to that of a benevolent supernatural deity which was believed to give its life willingly for the survival of the people to whom it offered its protection. As such, the bison was considered to possess power that could be called upon by the shamans (medicine men) during their invocations for aid, and symbols of the buffalo such as the shaved horns on this Blackfoot shaman's cap were used to create a spiritual link between the animal and the people.

The Plains and Prairies

RIGHT
This buckskin doll was made by a Sioux mother or grandmother for the enjoyment of a young girl. Like children everywhere, the sons and daughters of Plains Indians often emulated their parents in play and such a doll might well have featured in games of 'mothers and fathers'.

BELOW RIGHT
The semi-nomadic tribes of the Mississippi-Missouri often shaved their heads, leaving only a small ridge of hair across the top of the head to which a 'roach' headdress was attached by threading a long lock of hair, the scalplock, through a central hole and fixing it in place with a bone pin.

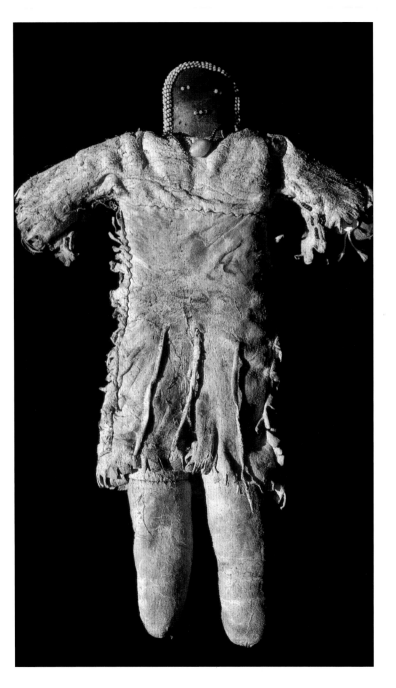

akapupapa'patdetk, 'my people who went to the Nez Percé are not wearing Nez Percé belts'. Typical of the Crow are stories of Old Man Coyote, an incorrigible buffoon and lecher who was believed to have created the earth. These obscene tales were related with relish before mixed audiences, although young girls – who were considered to be pure and innocent – were told not to listen.

Despite the lack of seriousness which marks Crow narratives, it is clear they were perfectly capable of defending their lands and were not a force to be trifled with. Crow determination to hold on to their lands and not to surrender to outside pressures is shown in this speech, made by a Crow warrior to Major Hatting at Cow Creek when it was announced that the boat containing food, goods, and annuities was to continue to Fort Pierce without unloading its goods in Crow territory.

> *I am not a chief, but I am a warrior. I see that my chiefs all hang their heads down waiting some reply from their father, as they do not know what to do or say. But I know what to do.* [Striking the table with his tomahawk he told the agents to] *hold up your heads when you speak to chiefs and warriors, look them in the eye! We suppose you must have some sense, or our Great Father would not have sent you here. My chiefs have spoken, but it seems they have not been heard. I tell you these goods were promised here, and they will go no further ... do you hear that? That is what I have to say as a warrior.*
>
> (Crow warrior to Major Hatting, June 1849)

The boat was unloaded.

ELOW

*fe on the Plains was often fraught with danger and
ncertainty and some form of spirit protection was
ught by all. Parents would give protection to a new-
rn child by preserving the umbilical cord and
rapping it in a decorative pouch that was attached to
e cradle while the child was an infant, then worn
til the child acquired more potent supernatural
sistance at puberty. The quilled container shown
re represents Turtle, a powerful and beneficient
pernatural that offered help and guidance to young
oux boys.*

BELOW

*The acquisition of horses and guns from Europeans
revolutionized Plains life and was largely responsible for
the 'warrior ideal' that developed within the grasslands.
Although used as utilitarian hunting and war weapons,
guns and gun cases were nevertheless subject to elaborate
decoration and ornamentation. The example shown here is
from the Crow.*

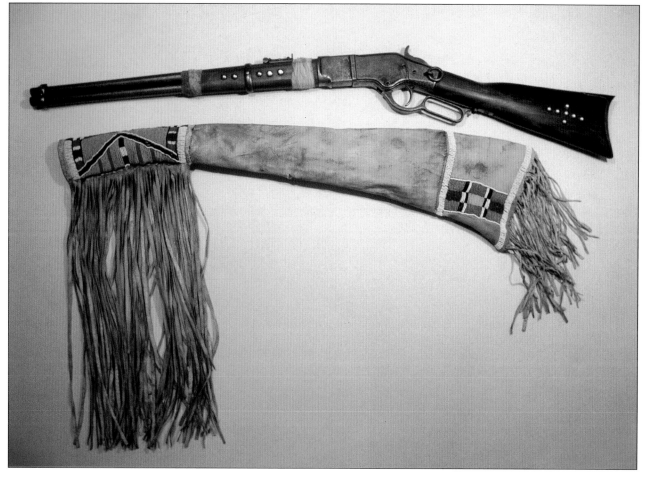

Cheyenne, Comanche, Kiowa and Kiowa-Apache

The southern Plains, which were home to such tribes as the Cheyenne, Comanche, Kiowa and Kiowa-Apache, include some of the earliest occupants of the grasslands as well as some of the most recent. The Cheyenne of southern Colorado and south-western Kansas did not leave Minnesota and enter the Plains much before 1700, when their economy changed virtually overnight from farming, gathering, and limited agriculture to a fully-fledged equestrian, buffalo-hunting culture; as for the Kiowa, there is little evidence that they ever lived outside the Plains. These tribes were among the first to be encountered by whites, since the exploratory parties sent out by the Spanish commander, Coronado, reported meeting wandering bands of nomadic hunters who relied on the dog for transportation of their goods and who fed on the flesh of the buffalo; these must have been the ancestors of the earliest Plains tribes and of the Plains Apache.

Strong band affiliation was a marked characteristic of these tribes, and each band operated as a political and economic unit under the leadership of a charismatic band chief. Some of these, normally comprising some 300 to 350 members, considered themselves to be autonomous units, able to act without tribal authority. The Dog-Soldiers of the Cheyenne, who were to cause so much havoc among the United States troops because of their unrelenting pursuit of Indian rights, were only one of these bands.

The Cheyenne Dog-Soldiers shared a 'no-flight' policy with some of the other Plains Warrior Societies, whereby they pledged never to retreat from battle but to continue fighting until they either achieved victory or were killed in the attempt. Because of this, they were among the fiercest and most persistent of warriors. Some of them wore long sashes which trailed behind them and which they would peg down in battle, refusing to move from the spot despite overwhelming odds unless they were ritually released by being touched by another member of the society.

Although the Dog-Soldiers were considered brave, it was the Kiowa-Apache, an Athapascan-speaking group to whom the Kiowa offered protection, who were renowned for the fact that they recognized that bravery rested with the individual and was not dependent on any supernatural assistance. No amount of supernatural protection could turn a coward into a brave warrior; although they believed in the general

Plains rule that medicine power protected the individual in his contests with enemies.

Irving, quoting Captain Bonneville, noted the religious beliefs of the Kiowa and commented that they:

> Were friendly in their dispositions, and honest to the most scrupulous degree in their intercourse with the white men. Simply to call these people religious would convey but a faint idea of the deep hue of piety and devotion which pervades the whole of their conduct. Their honesty is immaculate, and their purity of purpose, and their observance of the rites of their religion, are most uniform and remarkable. They are, certainly, more like a nation of saints than a horde of savages.

Although Bonneville found the Kiowa 'courteous and honest', the southern Plains tribes nevertheless came under the same pressures as those of their northern neighbours. Satanta, a prominent Kiowa chief, expressed this when he said:

> A long time ago this land belonged to our fathers; but when I go up to the river I see camps of soldiers on its banks. These soldiers cut down my timber; they kill my buffalo; and when I see them my heart feels like bursting. I feel sorry ... has the white man become a child that he should recklessly kill and not eat? When the red men slay game they do so that they may live and not starve.

The more humane face of the Kiowa and the Kiowa-Apache is shown in the fact that captured women and children were invariably

OPPOSITE LEFT

This photograph from the mid-1800s of an Osage warrior clearly shows the manner in which roach headdresses were worn.

OPPOSITE RIGHT

Plains men and women carried knives that were used as utilitarian objects and as defensive weapons. Although early knives were made from horn or bone, these were quickly replaced by metal trade knives such as those shown here. Decorated sheaths, formerly quilled and later embellished with trade beads, were used to house the knives and were worn attached to a belt around the waist.

BELOW

Warfare was endemic among Plains tribes, but was waged according to codes of honour and bravery that were deeply engrained and which accorded status to the individual who was prepared to place himself at risk through hand-to-hand encounters with an enemy. The Sioux club shown here was a close-contact weapon and has a flexible binding to the head which allows it to move and thereby increases the force of any blow that is delivered.

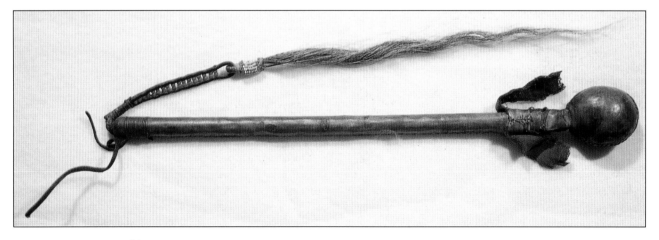

RIGHT

Plains warriors placed a high value on personal adornments and often traded widely for items that could not be obtained locally. This Crow necklace is made from shells which could only have been acquired through trade contact.

adopted into the tribes, where they were given the same status and accorded the same rights as women and children of their own blood. Even a captive white woman had exactly the same status as a full-blood Kiowa or Kiowa-Apache wife, and the tales of Indian atrocities towards their captives, which were rampant in the press of the time, were largely due to the over-heated imaginings of newspaper proprietors and the desire of a public which considered the 'Indian problem' to be due to savages who needed to be removed for the good of the United States.

Most of the Indian 'troubles' were not, however, the result of any particularly aggressive stance maintained by the Plains tribes. They were merely defending their way of life against the incursions of white hunters and settlers. Within their own communities they were loving, affectionate, and outgoing, although these were private matters and formal reserve on meeting strangers often made it difficult for outsiders to appreciate the fact. Yet it is clear that Kiowa and Kiowa-Apache children were often indulged as 'favourite sons' or 'favourite daughters' to the point where everything was done for them.

A favourite son might be protected from the dangers of the warpath through which others gained honours, and be pampered to the extent that he gained few skills in hunting or warfare. His status depended entirely on his relatives' ability to give gifts of horses to the poor and to hold outstanding feasts in his name. Although this cosseting of a favourite son is an extreme example, all children were encouraged to express themselves and to join in tribal affairs, the only punishment ever used being that of ignoring their demands.

A well-behaved child, that is one who showed respect for his or her elders, was honoured and considerable respect was shown for his or her achievements. Thus the boy's first successful attempt at hunting, although he may only have killed a rabbit, was marked by a feast to which the heads of the leading families, and even the chiefs and shamans, were invited. A girl's first attempt at beadwork, perhaps a shoulder strip that would be sewn onto a war shirt, was proudly displayed regardless of its actual quality.

Comanche

The Comanche, who were allied with the Kiowa, were perhaps the most nomadic of the Plains buffalo hunters. The name of one of the bands of the Nokoni Comanche translates as 'Wanderers' due to their habit of

making long journeys simply to 'see what is there'. Quanah Parker, a half-blood, but nevertheless the most vehement of the Comanche chiefs who declared war on Texas and the United States, was the son of a Nokoni chief.

Even their name attests to their free-ranging spirit, since it derives from the Ute word Komanchi, meaning 'Strangers', and refers to the appearance of Comanche warriors in the Great Basin territories that the Utes occupied. The translations of other band names also reflect the Comanche need to be constantly on the move: Making-Bags-While-

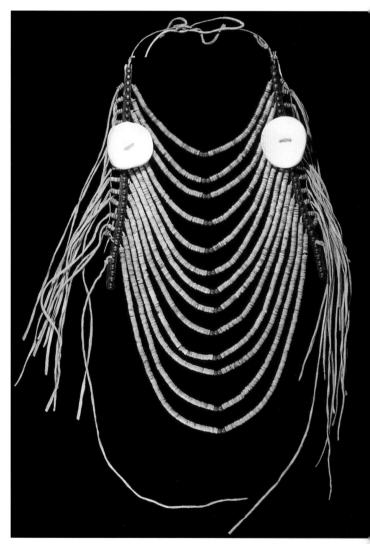

Moving, and Those-Who-Move-Often are typical.

The Comanche, like all the 'Horse Indians' of the Plains, were
killed equestrians. George Catlin, a painter and writer who had already
spent much time among the tribes of the Upper Missouri in the 1830s,
including the Sioux and Blackfoot, claimed the Comanche were the
most expert horsemen he had ever encountered. He wrote:

*Amongst their feats of riding, there is one that has astonished me
more than anything of the kind I have ever seen, or expect to see,
in my life: – a stratagem of war, learned and practised by every
young man in the tribe; by which he is able to drop his body upon
the side of his horse at the instant he is passing, effectually
screened from his enemies' weapons as he lays in a horizontal
position behind the body of his horse, with his heel hanging over
the horses' back; by which he has the power of throwing himself
up again, and changing to the other side of the horse if
necessary. In this wonderful condition, he will hang whilst his
horse is at fullest speed, carrying with him his bow and his
shield, and also his long lance of fourteen feet in length, all or
either of which he will wield upon his enemy as he passes; rising
and throwing his arrows over the horse's back, or with equal
ease and equal success under the horse's neck. This astonishing
feat which the young men have been repeatedly playing off to
our surprise as well as amusement, whilst they have been
galloping about in front of our tents, completely puzzled the
whole of us; and appeared to be the result of magic, rather than
of skill acquired by practice. Besides this wonderful art, these
people have several other feats of horsemanship, which they are
continually showing off; which are pleasing and extraordinary,
and of which they seem very proud. I am ready, without
hesitation, to pronounce the Camanchees the most extraordinary
horsemen that I have seen yet in all my travels, and I doubt very
much whether any people in the world can surpass them.*

But the Comanches, in common with other Plains tribes, were
destined to lose this freedom when they were confined on reservations
and forced to abandon or sell off their ancestral lands. In the Moon of
the Changing Season, October 1867, one of the most notable councils
took place at Medicine Lodge, Kansas, named as such because the
remains of a Sun Dance encampment, or Medicine Lodge, at which the

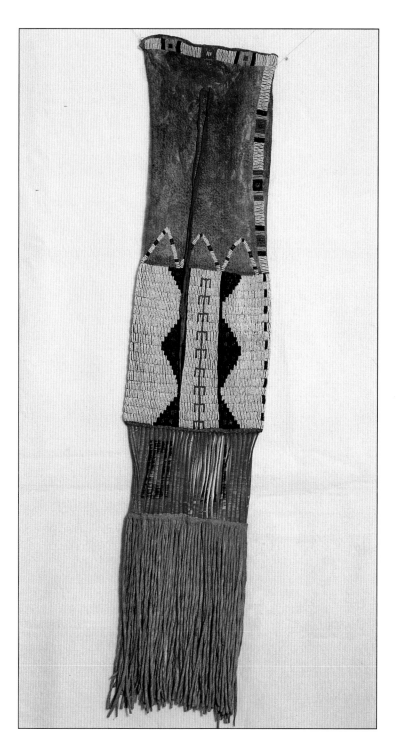

83

The Plains and Prairies

*Although rarely used for recreational purposes,
tobacco was widely applied during private and
public rituals and ceremonies as a means of
making contact with the spiritual powers. It was
believed that tobacco smoke made the breath
'visible' and acted as a link between the powers
of the earth and sky and between people and the
spirits. When not in use both pipe and tobacco
were kept in richly-decorated pipe bags such as
the Cheyenne or Sioux example shown here.*

The Plains and Prairies

people annually renewed their tribal allegiance, were still visible on the banks of the river.

Over 4,000 Indians, including representatives of the Arapaho, Cheyenne, Kiowa, Comanche, and Plains Apache, attended this council. They were asked to agree to the establishment of a reservation south of the Arkansas River. Parra-Wa-Samen, or Ten Bears, spoke for the Comanche:

> My heart fills with joy when I see you here, as the brooks fill with water when the snow melts in the spring; and I feel glad as the ponies do when the fresh grass starts in the beginning of the year. My people have never first drawn a bow or fired a gun against the whites. It was you who sent out the first soldier and we who sent out the second. The blue dressed soldiers and the Utes came from out of the night when it was dark and still, and for campfires they lit our lodges. Instead of hunting for game they killed my braves, and the warriors of the tribe cut their hair for the dead. They made sorrow come into our camps. The Comanches are not blind and weak. like the pups of dogs. They are strong and far-sighted, like grown horses. But there are things you have said to me which I do not like. They are not sweet like sugar, but bitter like gourds. You said you wanted to put us upon a reservation. I do not want them. I was born upon the prairie where the wind blew free and there was nothing to break the light of the sun. I was born where there were no enclosures and where everything drew a free breath. I want to die there and not within walls. Do not ask us to give up the buffalo for the sheep. The young men have heard talk of this and it has made them sad and angry. There might have been peace; but that which you say we must live on is too small. You have taken away the places where the grass grew thickest and the timber was the best. It is too late. We only wish to wander on the prairies until we die.

(Ten Bears, Yamparika Comanche, October 1867)

The Mississippi-Missouri Tribes

In addition to its nomadic population, the Plains and Prairies also supported a number of semi-nomadic tribes who lived along the Mississippi-Missouri. In the north, on the Upper Missouri, were the Mandan, Hidatsa, and Arikara, while further south along the Mississippi and its tributaries were such powerful tribes as the Pawnee and Osage. To the north, between the Mississippi and the Great Lakes were the Sauk and Fox.

All these groups spent at least part of the year hunting buffalo, when they followed a nomadic way of life and used tipis. At such times they were virtually indistinguishable from the nomadic groups. But they returned for part of the year to permanent village sites with substantial earth-lodges in the north and grass-covered domed houses in the south, and where they raised corn, beans, squash, sunflowers, and pumpkins.

Unlike many Plains tribes, most of those of the Prairie groups – with the notable exception of the Sauk and Fox – remained relatively friendly to the Americans who entered their territories, but were nevertheless fully part of the war complex of the Plains in their relations with other tribes. The Pawnee in particular were subject to continual raids from the Siouan tribes, who would lay siege to the Pawnee village or, if the Pawnee were away on their annual buffalo hunts, would destroy the fields of ripening crops. Many of the horses in Sioux camps were obtained by raiding the Pawnee pony herds; the Pawnee, in turn, travelled south to raid tribes such as the Kiowa. Pawnee optimism is reflected in the fact that horse raiders always left on foot, since they expected to return riding enemy ponies.

Friendship towards the whites did not result in favourable treatment and the Prairie tribes were eventually relocated on reservations in new regions and their original homelands broken up and opened to white settlement. More disastrously, however, their close contact with whites – which was occasioned by contacts due to their close proximity to the Mississippi-Missouri, which became a leading trade route into the interior – resulted in devastating epidemics that reduced their numbers and their fighting strength and left them vulnerable to attack by the nomadic groups.

This is nowhere more poignantly shown than among the Mandan. Their population in 1837 was estimated at 1600, but smallpox – perhaps intentionally introduced – reduced the entire tribe to only 31 in 1837.

The Plains and Prairies

Although men frequently rode bareback or with only a folded blanket as a saddle, longer rides were made more comfortable by using a 'pad saddle' such as this Crow example. Women's saddles, needed when transporting the family possessions when travelling from one campsite to another, more frequently had high cantles and pommels to which saddle bags and cradles could be attached.

The Plains and Prairies

The Plains tribes needed to travel about and therefore required numerous containers, such as this Sioux saddle bag, to carry items of everyday use as well as provisions. Such containers were often richly decorated and used as display items when the tribes were on the move.

Mato Tope, or Four Bears, a formidable warrior and chief but who had always offered friendship and protection to the whites, cursed the Americans as he lay dying from smallpox for the ravages that white diseases had caused among his people:

> *My Friends one and all, listen to what I have to say – Ever since I can remember, I have loved the Whites, I have lived With them ever since I was a Boy, and to the best of my Knowledge, I have never wronged a White man, on the Contrary, I have always Protected them from the Insults of Others, Which they cannot deny. The Four Bears never saw a White Man hungry, but what he gave him to eat, Drink, and a Buffaloe skin to sleep on, in time of Need. I was always ready to die for them ... and how have they repaid it! With ingratitude! I have Never called a White Man a*

Dog, but today, I do Pronounce them to be a set of Black Harted Dogs. They have deceived Me, them that I considered as Brothers, has turned out to be My Worst enemies. I have been in many Battles, and often Wounded, but the Wounds of my enemies I exalt in, but today I am Wounded, and by Whom, by those same White Dogs that I have always Considered, and treated, as Brothers. Listen well what I have to say, as it will be the last time you will hear Me. Think of your Wives, Children, Brothers, Sisters, Friends, and in fact all that you hold dear, are all Dead, or Dying, with their faces all rotten, caused by those Dogs the Whites.

(Mato Tope, or Four Bears, dying of smallpox, 30 July 1837)

The sense of being cheated and deceived by the Americans after showing them friendship is frequently expressed by the Prairie tribes. As the groups closest to white settlement and in the direct line of white expansion they became subject to encroachment upon their lands and subsequent demoralization at an earlier date than other Plains tribes. It is also very apparent that in their relations with the Americans the Prairie tribes had little to gain. White Shield, a prominent Arikara chief who respected the whites and who actually had some white blood in his family line and had always maintained friendly contact, cried out in despair during his old age when treaty goods that had been promised to the tribe in exchange for their lands failed to arrive.

> *I am old it is true; but not old enough to fail to see things as they are, and even, as you say, if I am now just an old fool, I would still prefer a hundred times to be a honest red fool than a thieving white scamp like you.*

(White Shield, Arikara Chief, 1867)

Yet even under these pressures the Prairie tribes held fast to values of respect and honesty among themselves and never lost their deep reverence for the natural powers by which they were surrounded. Even after their numbers had been more than halved by European diseases and their villages reduced to a fraction of what they had previously been, and despite continued pleas to the Americans to provide security from Sioux raids, the Pawnee never abandoned their beliefs in the powers of Morning and Evening Star and their poetic interpretations of the beings that inhabited the heavens and the earth. These were the immense forces that underlay every aspect of Pawnee thought.

Yet even Morning Star could not offer the assistance the Pawnee so desperately needed, and on numerous occasions they returned home from their annual buffalo hunts to find the fields flattened, the storage pits full of dried corn and buffalo meat for winter use ransacked, and the old people who had been left behind dead from Sioux attacks. With their numbers so seriously depleted, the Pawnee pleaded again and again with U.S. authorities to provide the protection they needed and which had been promised in their treaties, and each time were refused. Surprisingly the Pawnee kept their anger in check. At this time they were still the most feared tribe among southern Plains groups due to their continual raids into these territories, and it is clear that they could have proved very troublesome to the Americans had they chosen to resist.

Instead, they compromised. The Pawnee repeatedly made agreements with American authorities which the Pawnee kept but the Americans broke; and each time the Pawnee came back to the negotiations with renewed hope that this time the Americans would keep their word and provide the assurances and guarantees they had promised. None of these promises were kept, and today the Pawnee are one of the most impoverished tribes in the United States. The Pawnee commitment to living honestly and without dissemblance is summed up in this short statement by Horse Chief, which he made at the Fort Leavenworth Treaty in 1833 when the Pawnee agreed to cease hostilities against the Delaware; their true intentions were questioned by the commissioners, who felt the Pawnee might revert to raiding as soon as the treaty was concluded:

I have promised to the Delawares the friendship of my tribe. I respect my promise, and I cannot lie, for I am a Pawnee Chief.

Travelling was the traditional way of life on the Plains and Prairies and meant that few domestic utensils were made. Eating was mostly from wooden bowls or plates, and it was customary for each guest to supply his own. This Cheyenne horn spoon is typical of the Plains area and would have been the only utensil, other than a knife, which a guest would bring to a feast.

The Arctic and Subarctic

This vast region, comprising most of North America, from Labrador and Newfoundland in the east, to the Hudson Bay, and west to Alaska, and including the coastal regions of Greenland, and crossing the Canadian continent into Siberia, is the home of the Subarctic Athapascan and Cree and of the Arctic Eskimo. Although comprising nearly half the land mass of the North American continent, this region sustained only a tiny percentage of the aboriginal population. An estimated population density of one person per 100 square miles (259 sq km) is generally agreed among anthropologists.

Conditions here are harsh. Short summers and long winters, which in the far north result in a six-month season during which the sun never rises and everything is in perpetual twilight, did not permit the tribes to develop any real sense of solidarity. Resources were so few and so difficult to obtain that it was impossible to support large concentrations of people in any single area. As a consequence, most 'tribal' groups were, in reality, only a few individuals who were related through birth or marriage. These often consisted of as few as 20 or 30 people.

These extended family bands spent most of their time adapting to the seasonal flow of migratory animals, the thawing of rivers where fish could be caught, and the ripening of berries and other plant foods, and it was only on rare occasions that several bands met together for feasts and ceremonies which enabled them to demonstrate some form of tribal identity. These usually occurred in the spring and summer months, when climatic conditions were more favourable and when hunting or fishing had provided a sufficient quantity of food to support the feasts. Such feasts might last for only a few days, until the supply of food ran out,

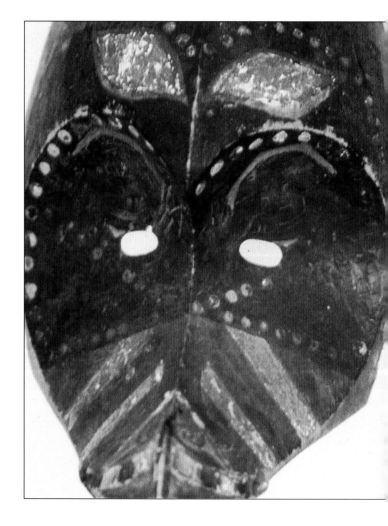

The Eskimo were highly skilled in adapting local materials to the harsh conditions of their Arctic environment. These mittens are made from seal gut and, although lightweight, provide an impermeable surface, preventing penetration by water.

Inuit (Eskimo) status was indicated by the use of labrets, or lip plugs, as shown in this group of prominent men from Icy Cape, photographed in about 1880. Small incisions were made in the lower lip at a name-giving ceremony in childhood, and these were gradually enlarged by the insertion of ivory plugs of increasing size at later ceremonies. The final size of the plug was the ultimate sign of the individual's importance in society.

LEFT

Athapascan tribes of the Yukon and Mackenzie river drainages in Alaska shared a similar life-style to that of the Eskimo. The mask shown here was made by the Ingalik and depicts Bear, a formidable foe but also the possessor of great supernatural power.

but at these times the people ate tremendous quantities and barely slept. Dancing and singing might be continued for 24 hours or longer, since this was the only opportunity for social gatherings.

Both the Arctic and Subarctic supported nomadic groups, primarily because the limited local resources were depleted rapidly and families were therefore forced to move about to ensure a continued food supply. The area is too far north for any agriculture or farming, and the precarious nature of life in these regions meant that periods of plenty, when inter-group activities took place, were few and far between. Much of the time the Arctic and Subarctic peoples lived on the edge of famine.

That the lives of these people were harsh and difficult is without doubt, yet there was also a certain romanticism that pervades the early reports of the Hudson's Bay Company representatives: the 'Bay' being the first contact these tribes had with western civilization. The remoteness of the region; the cool, clear, crystal lakes; the sense of endless freedom and a complete removal of any restrictions or barriers, all served to promote a sense of adventure and self-reliance. An individual survived in the Arctic and Subarctic on the strength of his or her wits, and this justifiably engendered a sense of pride and self-worth. This was no place for weakness or timidity.

Robert Ballantyne, who was apprenticed to the Hudson's Bay Company in the 1890s, wrote that:

Winter could not be expected to give up its dominion without a struggle. In October it began, and in November its empire was established. During December, January, February, March, and April, it reigned unmolested, in steadfast bitterness; enclosing in its icy bands, and retaining in torpid frigidity, the whole animate and vegetable creation. On the 12th of May, Hayes River, which had been covered for nearly eight months with a coat of ice upwards of six feet thick, gave way before the floods occasioned by the melting snow. The sublimity of the spectacle that met our gaze can scarcely be imagined. The noble river, here nearly two miles broad, was entirely covered with huge blocks and jagged lumps of ice, rolling and dashing against each other in chaotic confusion. In this state it continued for a week; and then, about the end of May, the whole floated quietly out to sea, and the cheerful river gurgled along its bed with many a curling eddy and watery dimple rippling its placid face. Although the river

was free, many a sign of winter yet remained around our forest home. The islands in the middle of the stream were covered with masses of ice, many of which were piled up to a height of twenty or thirty feet. All along the banks, too, it was strewn thickly; while in the woods snow still lay in many places several feet deep.

(Robert Michael Ballantyne; *Hudson Bay, or Everyday Life in the Wilds of North America*; 1897)

The irony of the Subarctic and Arctic is that in order to withstand intense cold it is necessary to consume large amounts of food, particularly fats, to ensure a requisite intake of calories and fatty acids that protect against low temperatures; yet recourse to animals that might provide these requirements was severely limited. Throughout much of the area the rabbit, or snowshoe hare, was common; but this animal has little body fat for much of the year and it was a common adage that 'one could starve to death on rabbits'.

Moose and caribou in the Subarctic areas, and seal in the Arctic, provided the main meat diet, although beaver were also trapped in the Subarctic regions. During periods of plenty, much of the meat was smoke-dried over fires as a quick method of preservation while travelling; although this only saved the meat for a few days. The slow drying of meat resulted in more lasting preservation but required a stay in camp of several days for the process to be completed. This was usually only possible during spring, when huge quantities of fish might be prepared in this way.

Despite the need for nomadism as the usual pattern of life, there were enforced periods of inactivity when conditions were too severe for travel or hunting. These encouraged the story-makers to recount tales of ancient experiences as a way of distracting attention from the severity of the environment. Family groups gathered in the shelter of a bark-covered wigwam or in an Eskimo igloo to listen to these tales of wisdom related by the oldest members of the group. That the same tales were repeated every winter did not detract from their value since they were accounts of how their ancestors had lived and still contained valuable insights into how life should be lived in the present.

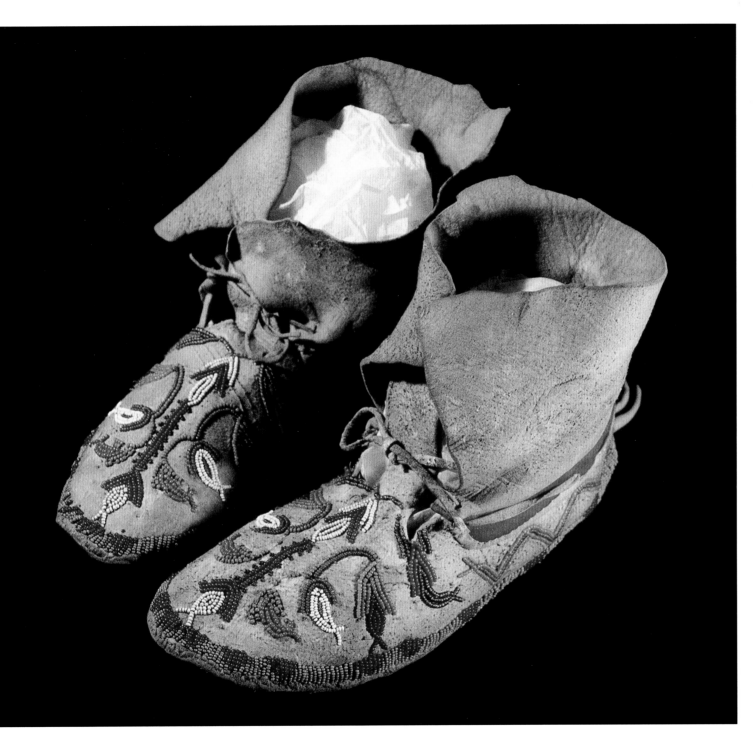

The Cree were the dominant force in the eastern Subarctic region and acted as 'middlemen' in the trade between Europeans based at Hudson's Bay and the Athapascan tribes to the west. High moccasins, such as the ones shown here, were characteristic of the Cree.

The Arctic and Subarctic

The Athapascans

The western half of the Subarctic area was occupied by numerous small bands belonging to the Athapascan linguistic stock. The principal tribes are the western Athapascans of the Yukon and Mackenzie living near and influenced by the Eskimo, among whom the dominant tribal groups are the Ingalik, Kutchin, Tanaina, and Koyukon; tribes living along the eastern foothills of the Rocky Mountains, which include the Kaska, Tahltan, Sekani, Tsetsaut, Mountain, Carrier, and Chilcotin; and Athapascans living in the region of the Great Slave and Great Bear Lakes, the Slave, Dog-Rib, Yellowknife, Chipewyan, Beaver, and Hare.

All these tribes lived in the northern forests which border the Barren Grounds, the tundra areas that separate the Subarctic from the Arctic, and adopted the generalized Subarctic pattern of nomadic hunting, fishing, and gathering. Some distinction can, however, be made between the most westerly of these groups, such as the Kutchin and Ingalik, and those of the interior, since the Yukon and Mackenzie provided sufficient resources for semi-permanent villages and more stable communities.

All the Athapascan tribes, or Dene (the People) as they refer to themselves, nevertheless shared a belief in the power of spirits and forces that directed every action of their lives. This was not conceptualized as a division between the forces of the natural and the supernatural, as on the Northwest Coast, and no distinction was made between matters of an everyday nature and those of more spiritual content. David Wheeler, who spent many months living with the Dog-Rib Indians north of Great Slave Lake, noted:

> It is hard to grasp the attitude of the Dog-Rib towards spiritual matters. One thing is quite evident. He makes absolutely no distinction between the natural and the supernatural. He asks a Lake to send him fair weather as simply as he asks a trader to give him a cup of flour. In either case the petition is sometimes granted, sometimes not, for no reason apparent to him. That their own ability to forecast the whereabouts of game was not due to clairvoyance but to experience and subconscious memory was an idea wholly foreign to their nature. It is far more natural for them to attribute their own success to strong medicine than to skill.

(David Wheeler, *The Dog-Rib Indian*, 1914)

A belief in spirit forces, or supernatural powers, was nevertheless

prevalent in Athapascan thought. Shamans, or 'Dreamers', were considered particularly potent and were believed to send their souls on out-of-body journeys during which they might converse with the shamans of another group and two shamans, even though physically separated by several hundred miles, might commune regularly. Curiously, although the bands were scattered and separated for much of the year, they always knew instinctively when an abundance of food was located in any particular area, and would gather together for celebrations. The Dene explain this as the result of dream communication.

Sharing of resources, both in times of plenty and of scarcity, is an Athapascan characteristic. Even a man who refuses to work will be fed and the sharing of meat is unconditional. Naeme Tuglavina expressed this when she said:

When anyone comes asking for something, I always give it, if I have it. It doesn't matter if they can't repay you. Ever since I can remember, my mother always used to tell me that, even if I did not have very much, as long as I had a bit to share, and saw someone without anything to eat, she would like me to share with them. That was how I was brought up. She would tell me that, no matter how little I had, if I saw another without food, I was to share mine.

This sense of communal sharing is evident in all aspects of Athapascan life. Although the Elders were respected for their age, knowledge, and wisdom, the societies were truly egalitarian ones. There was no institution of authority, no exercise of power, no hierarchy or inherited privilege, no chiefs or other leaders. Even the shaman, in this land where contact with the spirits was so important, was thought of simply as another specialist; someone with particular skills that others might not have, but with no particular power to control others. Thus, the shaman was considered to be expert in his or her field, just as a hunter who always managed to locate game was an expert in his.

It follows also that there were no laws and no means of enforcing them. Yet the Athapascans lived a life of harmony and co-operation. Theft, violence, greed were unknown to them. If someone killed meat then everybody ate, and if a lodge was being erected then everyone helped. There was nevertheless a tacit acceptance of individual skills. A hunting party consisting of several men might wait until one individual, recognized for his skills in hunting, decided to move in a certain direction. No questions were asked; it was a simple acceptance of following the person who knew best.

Similarly, if camp was being moved the decision might rest on the fact that a shaman had 'dreamed' of a better location. He would simply start travelling in this direction and others would follow. Wheeler noted that even without laws of any kind the Athapascans never quarrelled.

Part of this was due to the fact that the Athapascans lived in small family groups, and the interdependence created by blood and marriage ties resulted in a strong sense of loyalty; but it was also because hunting peoples have learned to listen and to acknowledge, respond to, and respect small clues that indicate what others may think. Thus it is said that 'the people have powers, but not power. They have expertise, but not authority'. One highly respected Athapascan Elder, responding to the question:

'You, the leaders, where are you going to lead us?', answered by saying 'We won't lead you anywhere ... A Dene leader doesn't lead anybody anywhere. You go where you want to go.'

BELOW
The Naskapi of Labrador were one of the most isolated tribes on the North American continent, but nevertheless managed to come under the influence of British military authorities. This is evident in the caribou-skin coat shown here, which has been tailored after the style of European frock-coats of the period.

The Cree

The eastern Subarctic is home to Algonquian-speaking tribes, the largest of which, occupying some three-quarters of the region, are the various bands of Cree Indians. Although sharing most of the characteristics of the Athapascan tribes to the west, the Cree, in general, were more tribally organized – with clearly-defined roles laid down for chiefs – and certainly more warlike.

Alexander Mackenzie, who travelled from Montreal through the Northwest between 1789 and 1793, described the warlike character of the Cree:

Many and various are the motives which induce a [Cree] to engage in war. To prove his courage, or to revenge the death of his relations, or some of his tribe, by the massacre of an enemy. If the tribe feel themselves called upon to go to war, the elders convene the people, in order to know the general opinion. If it be for war, the chief publishes his intention to smoke in the sacred stem at a certain period, to which solemnity, meditation and fasting are required as preparatory ceremonials.When the people are thus assembled, and the meeting sanctified by the custom of smoking, the chief enlarges on the causes which have called them together, and the necessity of the measures proposed on the occasion. He then invites those who are willing to follow him, to smoke out of the sacred stem, which is considered as the token of enrolment; and if it should be the general opinion, that assistance is necessary, others are invited, with great formality, to join them. Every individual who attends these meetings brings something with him as a token of his warlike intention, or as an object of sacrifice, which, when the assembly dissolves, is suspended from poles near the place of council.

(Mackenzie; *Voyages from Montreal*)

Much of Cree aggression was originally vented against the neighbouring Athapascan tribes, particularly the Chipewyan, and seems to have been focused on stealing women; although many Chipewyan tales also tell of the Cree coming as 'strangers' from the far east and of being intruders who pushed some of the other tribes out of their original territories. Other factors also contributed. The formation of larger settlements, for instance, enabled the Cree to form war parties of relatively significant size and to rely on the assistance of allies.

Generally war was small-scale, and conducted as infrequent surprise raids when superiority in numbers made victory a virtual certainty. History, too, plays its part in determining Cree aggression. They received guns as early as the late 1600s, and even these weapons were sufficient to enable the Cree to expand into lands defended only by warriors with bows and arrows.

In addition, the Cree were in early contact with white traders, which not only permitted them to obtain better and more efficient weapons and to maintain a stock of ammunition, but enabled them to establish themselves as middlemen in the fur trade. Thus, later raiding was frequently intended to secure furs from neighbouring groups, which could be added to those their own hunters brought in. It was important, too, that the Cree prevented as much direct contact between the

RIGHT

Arctic regions, although inhospitably cold, were nevertheless remarkably dry. Even so, it was essential to safeguard against penetration by damp which would immediately freeze. The Eskimo bag shown here is made from seal gut that is impervious and sewn so that no stitches come through to the outer surface where they could enable damp to enter.

thapascans and the traders as possible, since this ensured the benefits of trading remained exclusively their own and prevented the thapascans from obtaining weapons in trade with which they might etaliate.

It should not, however, be thought that war was a constant reoccupation of the Cree. The poor weather conditions for much of the ear actually made war impossible except for a relatively brief period in he summer when travel was easy, and for much of the year Cree living as virtually indistinguishable from that of the tribes to their west. They ad the same beliefs in the powers of their shamans and in a multitude f spirit forces that inhabited the forests and which could exert either nalevolent or benevolent power; the only possible exception being the ree belief that, above all, these powers emanated from one single reator figure or Manitou.

At some point around 1820, some Cree bands began to move out of he southern parts of the Subarctic region into the northern Great Plains a quest for game, especially buffalo, and where they came into contact and conflict – with Plains tribes. These bands, however, adopted a umber of Plains traits, particularly the use of the horse (for which they bandoned their former mode of canoe travel) and are known as the lains Cree. Although retaining a number of Woodland features in their ulture, they became virtually indistinguishable from other northern lains tribes.

Montagnais-Naskapi

rief mention needs to be made of the Algonquian-speaking tribes of he far eastern Subarctic, north of the St. Lawrence and in Labrador. hese are the Montagnais-Naskapi, two groups with a virtually identical ulture. Unlike their linguistic relatives, the Cree, the Montagnais-laskapi had no political unit above the simple family band, and no hiefs. Like the Athapascans they were a peaceful and docile people ho sought no hostile relations with their neighbours.

The unfavourable habitat in which they lived undoubtedly ontributed to this, since there was little possibility for large groups to orm and little reason to raid a neighbouring group. The Cree desire to apture enemy women could not have provided an impetus for warfare ere, since the winter is so severe that even a small family group often aced starvation and by increasing its numbers a group would simply

have made it more difficult to obtain the resources needed for survival.

Much emphasis was again placed on spiritual forces and the ability of the shamans to bring these to the aid of the people. Much of the shamanic tradition rested on foretelling the future and bringing game, and was often practised in the form of scapulmancy, when the shoulder blade of an animal, often a caribou, since caribou were the prime food source in this area, was heated in the fire until it cracked. By reading the pattern of the cracks and burn marks, predictions about the weather and the location of game animals were made.

LEFT

Snowshoes were an essential winter requirement of tribes living in the Subarctic regions, and were designed to spread the weight of the wearer over a larger surface, thereby preventing him from sinking into the soft snow. They were not used by the Eskimo in the far north where freezing conditions rarely resulted in soft snow underfoot that would have been a hindrance to travel.

BELOW

Resources were scarce in the far north and the Inuit (Eskimo) managed to display a great deal of ingenuity in adapting virtually anything to a practical use. The pouch shown here has been made from a pelican beak.

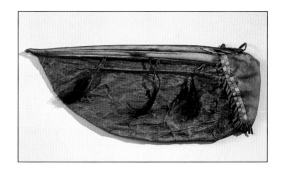

The Arctic and Subarctic

ABOVE

The difficulties of living in the Arctic and Subarctic regions meant that people looked to beneficent supernatural powers to help them cope with the harsh conditions surrounding them. Among the Eskimo, shamans (medicine men) were particularly prominent and wore distinguishing items of dress, such as the shaman's cap shown here.

RIGHT

To the south of the Inuit, in the forested regions of Subarctic Canada, elm and birch bark were valuable commodities and used for everything, from covers for wigwams and outer skins of canoes to containers and bags. The Athapascan elm-bark basket shown here would have been used either as a container for small items that could easily be mislaid, or as a cooking pot for preparing soups by filling with water and dropping in hot stones to heat the contents.

Eskimo and Aleut

North of the Subarctic, ranging through the tundra and snow regions located primarily, but not entirely, above the northern tree-line, from Greenland in the east through the Canadian territories and into Alaska and parts of Siberia, is the home of the Eskimo. Their linguistic relatives, the Aleut, who share a very similar culture, lived on the chain of small islands that stretch out from the Alaskan Peninsula into the Bering Sea and which are named after them: the Aleutian Islands.

Although the entire culture area is often referred to as Eskimo, there are actually three distinct groups: the Aleut, the Yupik Eskimo of Siberia and parts of Alaska, and the Inuit Eskimo. Modern Eskimos frequently refer to themselves collectively as Inuit, meaning 'The People', rather than using the term Eskimo which is an Algonquian Indian name for them and translates as 'Raw Meat Eaters'.

The region these tribes occupied has often been referred to as the harshest and most extreme environment inhabited by mankind. It is intensely cold: temperatures may rise only slightly above freezing in June, July, and August, and in January can fall to -22°F (-30°C) or lower. For the Eskimo, however, cold was a blessing; they had learned to live with the weather, not to fight it, and utilized cold as a means of survival. Crucial to this is the fact that although very cold, the Arctic is nevertheless dry. Problems of damp clothing that might freeze, which was of real concern to the survival of the Indians of the Subarctic during the winter months, was not a problem for the Eskimo.

Cold weather made transport easy, using sleds whose runners were brushed with water which instantly froze to provide a frictionless contact with the ice; animals left tracks and were easy to locate. The characteristic snow-house, or igloo, of the central Eskimo, which was used as a winter dwelling and often built far out on sea-ice, demonstrates how cold could be turned to advantage. The igloo was constructed from blocks of wind-packed snow, and when closed and heated from within by oil lamps caused a slight melt which instantly froze again on exposure to cold air. Such a dwelling could be erected in about an hour and would easily withstand the weight of a polar bear.

Winter dwellings in other areas were usually constructed from a conglomeration of materials – stone, bone, and turf were particularly popular – which was piled up to form a crude form of hut, and surrounded by blocks of snow to provide further insulation, some of

which were partly subterranean. Summer, which was a difficult time for the Eskimo, since sleds would not run smoothly over partially thawed tundra, was spent tracking animals on foot, relying on easily portable sealskin lodges.

Eskimo ingenuity in the use of local resources ensured wind- and damp-proof clothing. They manufactured clothing from the skins of caribou, seals, and even fish, as well as seal intestines, and wore two or three layers to trap air and provide insulation against the cold. Clothing was sewn in such a way that stitches never penetrated to the outside of the skins so that, when worn, they presented a surface impervious to the elements. Both Eskimos and Aleuts utilized every part of the animals, birds, and fish they killed. What was not used for food or clothing was converted into housing, sleds, kayaks (one man hunting boats) and umiaks (larger communal boats).

In the treeless Arctic, wood was a rarity and only to be obtained in the form of driftwood. It was therefore a precious commodity, never to be used as fuel, only in the manufacture of goods. Eskimos sleds, for instance, were often made from many relatively small pieces of

riftwood that were shaped and then fastened together with rawhide
indings. Fuel, both for heating and cooking, was invariably seal oil and
tone 'lamps' were a regular feature of every Eskimo household.
Iollowed out to create a depression which would hold the oil, and with
 floating wick of moss, these lamps provided heat, light, and warmth.

Yet despite the ingenuity and adaptability of the Eskimo and Aleut,
fe in the Arctic regions was always unpredictable. A shaman's
remonition that game was to be found in a certain area might prove
ncorrect, or a sudden storm (or 'white-out'), when wind-driven snow
bliterated everything and made it impossible to know in which
irection one was travelling, could overtake a family band as they
noved from one locality to another. Resources were often scarce, and
xposure at these latitudes without sufficient shelter or food would prove
atal within hours.

The harshness of Arctic life suggests that the Eskimo and Aleut
vere similarly cruel and unforgiving. Food was scarce and when the
ossible presence of game came to their notice, demanding fast action,
hose likely to impede the movement of the group were frequently left
ehind. Thus very young children, elderly people, and the sick, who
vould have had difficulty keeping up with the hunters, might be left to
lie. In these regions death from exposure came quickly and with little
ain. Though harsh, this reflects the Eskimo-Aleut philosophy that
urvival of the group over the individual was of paramount importance.

Many speeches reflect the agony suffered by people in these
ircumstances. They were family-oriented groups and most of their lives
vere spent in contact with only a few closely-related people with strong
ies to one another. The anguish of leaving a sickly mother or father
ehind, or a new-born child, can scarcely be imagined. Tears of sorrow,
f pity, and of helplessness accompanied these departures. Often the
lderly would plead with their relatives to leave them, realizing they
vere a burden which could result in the destruction of them all.

Leave me, leave me. I am old and have done my share. I can no
longer travel and am a burden to others. I have lived long and
am satisfied. Leave me, leave me. I have done my share and no
longer wish to live.

(Eskimo Elder, sacrificing his own life for the welfare of others)

The sentiments of the Eskimo are also expressed in this woman's
ong. While picking berries during the summer she is suddenly stricken
by memories of the loved ones she had left behind during the winter
months, and to whom she would normally have carried her berries first.
Realizing they are dead, and looking down on the calm waters in which
kayaks floated on the quiet seas, she voices her sadness:

Great grief came over me.
Great grief came over me.
While on the fell above us I was picking berries,
Great grief came over me.
My sun quickly rose over it.
Great sorrow came over me.
The sea out there off our settlement
was beautifully quiet.
And the great, dear paddlers
were leaving out there.
Great grief came over me
while I was picking berries on the fell.

Yet, despite the difficulties of their lives, the Eskimo-Aleut fought
back with humour. The rare occasions when several family groups came
together were marked with laughter and celebration that could last for
days. Food was consumed in vast quantities without thought of harsher
times to come.

Although life was difficult it was not impossible if met with
fortitude and resilience. Both Eskimo and Aleut rejoiced in the freedom
the Arctic gave them, while at the same time recognizing its restrictions.
They had no awareness of a past or future that was more important than
the present. One day was lived at a time for no one could know what the
next day might hold and the future was in any case always insecure.

The joy of the immediate is shown (right) by an Eskimo taking his
kayak out into the open seas on a fine day and expressing his pleasure in
finding the seas calm and tranquil.

The paddler's reference to his drum-song is the Eskimo way of
achieving redress through a poetry competition. Satirical verse was
employed before an audience who indicated their approval or
disapproval. Such *nith* or contention songs were recorded as early as
1746. When a person decided that someone has offended him, he would
compose a ridicule song and he and the accused would meet in a singing
match at which the laughter generated by each of their songs would
decide who was in the right. They would sing songs at each other until

When I'm out of the house in the open
I feel joy.
When I get out on the sea
I feel joy.
If it is really fine weather
I feel joy.
If the sky really clears nicely
I feel joy.
May it continue thus
for the joy of my sealing.
May it continue thus
for the joy of my hunting.
May it continue thus
for the joy of my singing.
May it continue thus
for the joy of my drum-song.

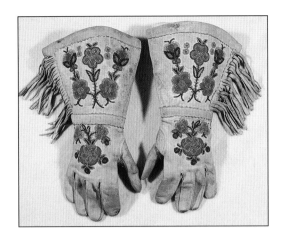

Warm clothing was a vital prerequisite of Subarctic life, since winter temperatures were so low as to immediately freeze any exposed part of the body. The heavy mittens shown here were made by the Cree.

the audience made their verdict known. Fearful of being shamed, the guilty party might very well retire, fearful of being the butt of the people's jokes.

This is not to suggest that Eskimo and Aleut were devoid of aggression. Those living in the southern interior who ventured into the Subarctic areas in spring and summer during their caribou hunts had, in fact, gained a reputation for their fierceness and uncompromising hostility towards the Athapascan tribes with whom they came in contact, and there were frequent conflicts between Aleut and Yupik Eskimo with tribes of the Northwest Coast. Usually, however, both Eskimo and Aleut were peace-loving and affable people.

Their greatest fear was not a hostile encounter with another tribe but the unpredictable nature of their environment, and this gave rise to a belief in a host of malevolent spirits that dwelt in the mists just beyond their line of vision. The most important power, nevertheless, dwelt in the depths of the sea. This was Sedna, the Mistress of the Animals, who, when angered by a breach of etiquette or taboo, would entice the animals away so that people could not find them and would starve.

The cause of Sedna's wrath was that when she lived as a human being she was married to Raven, a match of which her father disapproved. Her father stole her back, but was pursued by Raven when making off with her in his kayak. Raven flew low over the water, beating the waves with his wings until a terrible storm threatened to swamp the boat. In desperation Sedna's father threw her overboard. Sedna tried to climb back into the kayak, but her father chopped off her fingers which were grasping the gunwale of the boat. She descended to the bottom of the sea. When people break the laws she has set them, her hair becomes tangled and matted but, without fingers, she is unable to comb it out and this makes her angry.

Only shamans can intercede and beg Sedna's forgiveness. By entering a trance, the shaman sends his 'soul' on an out-of-body journey to Sedna's abode where, with gentle words and soft caresses, he attempts to soothe Sedna's temper by combing her hair. If successful, Sedna will remove the blanket with which she has covered the animals and release them, informing the shaman where they may be found.

An interesting aspect of the shaman's trance is that it acts as a 'confessional' for the people. The shaman asks everyone to confess any sins they may have committed. These can range from adultery to the crime of eating the meat of sea and land animals together, since these should never be mixed. By confessing their crimes publicly they can be forgiven, and it is a notable aspect of Eskimo life that grudges are rarely held, even when the crime is conceived as being the cause of starvation. The Eskimo and Aleut are forgiving people who realize that wrongdoing is inevitable but, as long as it is admitted, can be pardoned. Only those refusing to admit their failings cannot be forgiven.

The self-effacing attitude of the Eskimo is reflected in the shaman's demeanour during these seances. The Arctic explorer, Knud Rasmussen, witnessed several shamanic events and has recorded them in detail. At one of these the shaman, Kigiuna, attempted to calm a storm that was making it impossible for the people to leave their homes. They were starving because they were unable to secure meat, so Kigiuna appealed to Sedna:

> *Woman, great woman down there,*
> *Send it hence, send it away from us, that evil!*
> *Come, come, spirit of the deep!*
> *One of your earth-dwellers*
> *Calls to you.*
> *Asks you to bite enemies to death.*
> *Come, come, spirit of the deep!*

In a terrific struggle, Kigiuna and another shaman, Baleen, acted out a battle between the storm spirits. Rasmussen records the ecstasy of the people who witnessed this scene and of his own 'loss of sense' when Baleen gripped Kigiuna by the throat and brutally flung him back and forth among the crowds of spectators until Kigiuna lost consciousness. But when Kigiuna recovered it was he who seized Baleen, and choked the life from him. With his foot on the defeated Baleen's chest Kigiuna, trembling with emotion, declaimed:

> *The sky is full of naked beings rushing through the air. Naked people, naked men, naked women, rushing along and raising gales and blizzards. Don't you hear the noise? It swishes like the beats of the wings of great birds up in the air. It is the fear of naked people, it is the flight of naked people! The weather spirit is blowing the storm out, the weather spirit is driving the sweeping snow away over the earth, and the helpless storm-child Narssuk shakes the lungs of the air with his weeping. Don't you hear the weeping of the child in the howling of the wind? My*

*helping spirit will stop him, will stop them all. I see him coming
calmly, confident of victory, toward me. He will conquer, he will
conquer.*

Following this tremendous battle with the storm spirits, Kigiuna
announced that the storm would abate. Rasmussen and his companions
struggled back to their lodgings through driving snow and wind that
made it almost impossible to stand upright. They were sceptical about
Kigiuna's prediction, although all the Eskimo seemed convinced that
Kigiuna was right. We can only imagine Rasmussen's surprise when, on
waking the following morning, the storm had died down and the day
was dawning with glorious sunshine and fine weather.

Rasmussen also tells us of the shamans' denigration of their own
powers. Kigiuna had told him that what he was about to perform was
only 'a tissue of lies', and at another seance, held by the shaman Sorqaq,
Rasmussen's close friend, Peter Freuchen, was told:

*This is nothing for the great white man to look at. I am a big liar,
and even if these fools [the Eskimo] are stupid enough to believe
me, I could never deceive you, and your presence will embarrass
me. What happens here has nothing to do with the truth.*

Freuchen recorded his experiences at this seance, during which he
says sealskins 'crackled' through the air of their own volition.
Freuchen, as sceptical as Rasmussen, attempted to catch one of these
and received a blow that almost broke his arm; it was several weeks
before his injuries healed. At the end of the seance Sorqaq opened his
eyes and looked at Freuchen, who was carefully nursing his badly-
injured arm. Sorqaq smiled and said:

*Just lies and tricks.
The wisdom of our ancestors is not in me.
Do not believe in any of it!*

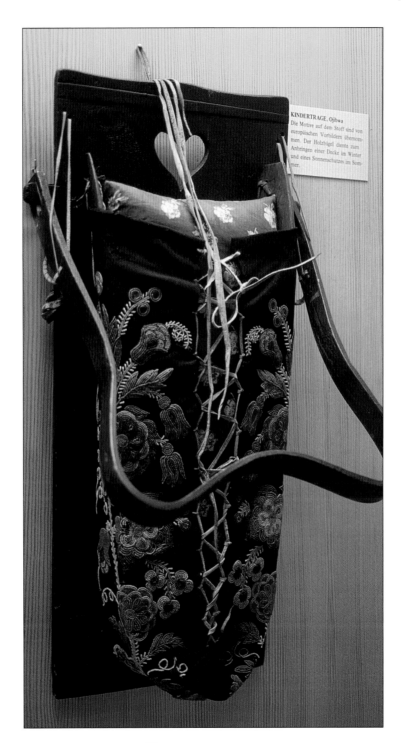

*Nomadic life-styles of the Subarctic meant that
infants needed to be protected. The Cree
cradleboard shown here was carried by means of
a strap which was looped across the mother's
shoulders. Such rigid cradleboards ensured that
the child was protected from accidental injury
while travelling through forests.*

The Eastern Woodlands

The eastern parts of the United States and Canada beyond the line of the Mississippi primarily consisted of forests and woodlands. These varied from coniferous forests in the north, deciduous forests in the central regions, and tropical swamplands of mangroves and cypresses in the south. The tribes living in these areas, although varying considerably in culture and beliefs, were all dependent on permanent village sites and on the cultivation of crops, except for those in the very far north who relied on wild rice as a staple food.

Villages often consisted of large communal buildings, or longhouses, surrounded by stockades, or, further south, of massive ceremonial temple-mound complexes. All the tribes in this region gained a reputation for being warlike and aggressive, although it is clear from the early Colonists' reports that they were greeted with friendly overtures and were only able to survive their first winters in the New World as a consequence of the help and assistance they received from the indigenous occupants of the lands to which they had come.

Chief Powhatan, who was instrumental in the successful founding of the first Colony, Jamestown, in 1607, soon came into conflict with James Smith's Colonists, who decided to burn down a large acreage of Powhatan hunting-grounds in order to grow tobacco – a skill which the Powhatan had taught them. Peace was restored through the intervention of Powhatan's daughter, Pocahontas, but the chagrin of Powhatan, who had hoped to achieve a peaceful co-existence with the Colonists, is clearly shown in this speech he made in 1609:

Why will you take by force what you may obtain by love? Why will you destroy us who supply you with food? What can you get by war? We are willing to give you what you ask, if you come in a friendly manner. I am not so simple as to not know it is better to eat good meat, sleep comfortably, live quietly with my women and children, laugh and be merry with the English, and being their friend, trade for their copper and hatchets, than to run away from them. Take away your guns and swords, the cause of all our jealousy, or you may die in the same manner.

(Powhatan, Algonquian Chief, Werowocomico [Gloucester County] 1609)

The principle tribes of this region were the Micmac and Beothuk in Newfoundland, the various Algonquian- and Iroquoian-speaking tribes of the central areas, the Natchez and the Five Civilized Tribes (Creek, Cherokee, Chickasaw, Choctaw, and Seminole) of the south, and the Timucua, Calusa, and Apalachee of Florida.

Although these tribes were quite diverse, they all shared a sense of living within regions that defined and limited movement. Unlike the Plains, where space is boundless, that of the Woodlands is restricted by trees and passage through the forests could often only be made by canoe along narrow rivers and channels. It was frequently impossible to know what lay beyond the next bend of the river or beneath the overhang of foliage that bent down to the water's edge, and this lent a certain sense of mystery to the Indians' relationship with their environment.

Every part of the land, whether it be tree, river, shaded grove, or orest clearing, was believed to be inhabited by spirits which could onfer benefits but which, if angered, could bring disaster. For the orthern tribes, the most important of these was the Thunderbird, which ppeared in people's lives as the eagle. When the Thunderbird flashed is eyes, lightning struck the ground, and when he folded his wings it ounded like a thunderclap.

For the tribes living near the Great Lakes, Thunderbird was onsidered to be in continual conflict with the Underwater Panther. heir tremendous battles manifested themselves in sudden storms or wift and unexpected currents that swept canoers to their deaths. All the ribes of the Woodlands were under the influence of these powerful upernatural forces which are depicted in the *Walam Olum* – the sacred ribal history of the Leni Lenape, or Delaware, whom many of the tribes onsidered to be 'Grandfathers': that is, respected ancestors and ancient ccupants of the region.

Long ago there was a mighty snake and beings evil to men. This mighty snake hated those who were there and greatly disquieted those whom he hated. They both did harm, they both injured each other, both were not in peace. Driven from their homes they fought with this murderer. The mighty snake firmly resolved to harm the men. He brought three persons, he brought a monster, he brought a rushing water. Between the hills the water rushed and rushed, dashing through and through, destroying much. Nanabush, the Strong White One, grandfather of beings, grandfather of men, was on the Turtle Island. There he was walking and creating, as he passed by and created the turtle. Beings and men all go forth, they walk in the floods and shallow waters, downstream thither to the Turtle Island. There were many monster fishes, which ate some of them. The Manitou daughter, coming, helped with her canoe, helped all, as they came and came. And also Nanabush, Nanabush, the grandfather of all, the grandfather of beings, the grandfather of men, the grandfather of the turtle. The men were then gathered on the turtle, like to turtles. Frightened on the turtle, they prayed on the turtle that what was spoiled should be restored. The water ran off, the earth dried, the lakes were at rest, all was silent, and the mighty snake departed.

(Leni Lenape *Walam Olum* or Red Score)

The Eastern Woodlands

Micmac and Beothuk

The Micmac and Beothuk were among the first of the Native Americans to come under pressure from European invaders of their lands. Originally hunters and gatherers, with a dependency on birch-bark canoes for transportation, they lived on the coastal regions of Newfoundland and of the Maritime Provinces of Canada.

Although they hunted deer and other animals in the forests, much of their economy was centred on the gathering of shellfish collected in coastal waters. They were mentioned by John Cabot in 1497 who remarked that they were a non-agricultural people who very much relied on their canoes and on catching fish. The Micmac, he notes, consisted of a group of seven tribes whose name translates as 'The Allies'.

Their contact with Europeans was to prove fatal to the Beothuk. Both the Micmac and the Beothuk became embroiled in the French and English disputes over control of the Colonial territories that lasted from 1689 until 1759. The Micmac were consistently friendly towards the French but against the English settlers, whereas the Beothuk sided with the English.

But British protection of the Beothuk, despite their resistance to French sympathy with the Micmac, was ineffectual. When the French offered scalp bounties to the Micmac and supplied them with guns, it roused ancient feelings of hostility and suspicion and the Micmac swarmed into Beothuk territory. Within a generation the tribe became virtually extinct. The last-known Beothuk, an elderly man who had escaped to the north as a boy and settled with the Naskapi in Labrador, died in 1829.

Yet it is clear that the Micmac were not entirely satisfied with their connections with the French, whom they thought of as an inferior race of human beings. As early as 1676, before the English-French conflicts, a Micmac chief chastised the French thus:

Thou reproachest us very inappropriately, that our country is a little hell on earth in contrast with France, which thou comparest to a terrestrial paradise, inasmuch as it yields thee, so thou sayest, every kind of provision in abundance. Thou sayest of us also that we are the most miserable and most unhappy of all men, living without religion, without manners, without honour, without social order, and in a word, without any rules, like the beasts in our woods and forests, lacking bread, wine, and a

thousand other comforts, which thou hast in superfluity in Europe. I beg thee now to believe that, all miserable as we seem in thy eyes, we consider ourselves nevertheless much happier than thou, in this that we are very content with the little that we have. Thou deceivest thyselves greatly if thou thinkest to persuade us that thy country is better than ours. For if France, as thou sayest, is a little terrestrial paradise, art thou sensible to leave it? Learn now, my brother once and for all, because I must open to thee my heart: there is no Indian who does not consider himself infinitely more happy and powerful than the French.
(Micmac Chief, 1676)

Algonquin and Iroquois

The central part of the Woodlands, from east of the Great Lakes to the Atlantic coast and extending through New York state and New England, Pennsylvania, and Virginia, is considered typical of the culture area. It is nevertheless clear that the Algonquian-speaking tribes, such as the Powhatan mentioned earlier, were ancient inhabitants of the region and that the Iroquois had moved in from further south. During these movements many of the Algonquin were forced out of their original homelands under the incursions of the Iroquois.

Both Iroquois and Algonquin shared a similar life-style based on permanent villages surrounded by fields sown with crops of corn, beans, and squash. These fields were formed by the slash-and-burn technique of agriculture in which trees were first felled and the area burned prior to planting. As the fields became exhausted, new ones were cleared until eventually they became too distant from the village for practical purposes making it necessary to relocate to a more central position.

Hunting was important too, and whereas the daily task of tending the fields was women's work, that of hunting was an exclusively male preserve. The main animal hunted was the deer, and in the early period all clothing was made from deerskins, although early contact with the French and English soon introduced cloth and this replaced much of the skin clothing. This division of labour was explained by the fact that the Spirits of the Three Sisters (corn, squash, and beans) were female, as was Mother Earth.

Women nevertheless had an important role to play and, especially among the Iroquois, a man on marriage went to live in the clan house of his wife. The matriarchs of the tribes, the Clan Mothers, also had a strong voice in tribal decision-making and government. Thus among the League of Five Nations, a group of Iroquois tribes organized for defence and offence, a council of ten men for each tribe voted on decisions that affected the Five Nations as a whole. It should be borne in mind that the council actually represented matrilineal clans and the members of the council were nominated by and reported back to a female constituency.

Algonquin government, by contrast, was often under charismatic leaders – the Powhatan, in fact, are named after Chief Powhatan, and like the Iroquois were a confederacy of different tribes who acted together in the common interest. The nature of these confederacies was nevertheless less stable than the Iroquois League, and as a consequence the numerically inferior Iroquois, by combined effort, defeated, and sometimes destroyed, much larger Algonquin forces.

The most characteristic feature of Iroquois and Algonquin relationships was mutual hostility. The Algonquins naturally resented Iroquois intrusions and, before the formation of the Five Nations, or 'People of the Long-house', were often able to hold off Iroquois attacks. They were all eventually pushed to the periphery of Five Nations country. Much of Five Nations aggression was nevertheless directed at other tribes speaking dialects of the same Iroquoian language as themselves.

The League of Five Nations was meant to prevent internecine warfare from weakening the tribes to the extent that they would have been unable to defend themselves. The League – which was founded by an idealistic young man named Hiawatha, together with an astute Iroquois law-maker named Daganawe da, and Jogan Sasay who was a

respected Clan Mother – consisted, from west to east, of the Seneca, Cayuga, Onondaga, Oneida, and Mohawk.

Hiawatha's dream was of an everlasting peace in which weapons would only be used in defence, and when Daganawe da announced the formation of the League the law-maker said:

I am Daganawe da, and with the Five Nations confederate lords I plant the Tree of the Great Peace ... I name the tree the Tree of the Great Long Leaves. Under the shade of this Tree of the Great Peace we spread the soft white feather down of the globe thistle as seats for you, Atotarho, and your cousin lords ... Roots have spread out from the Tree, and the name of these roots is the Great White Roots of Peace. If any man of any nation shall show a desire to obey the laws of the Great Peace, they shall trace the roots to their source, and they shall be welcomed to take shelter beneath the Tree of the Long Leaves. The smoke of the confederate fire shall pierce the sky so that all nations may discover the central council fire of the Great Peace.

(Deganawe da, founder of the League of Five Nations, 1570)

Yet despite the rhetoric of Daganawe da's speech, the Iroquoian-speaking Huron (Tobacco), Erie (Neutrals), and Susquehanna (Conestoga) refused to join and within a few short years became the focus of Five Nations aggression. This was at first directed primarily at the Huron, who had already formed a league of their own and wanted nothing to do with the Five Nations. Huron successes were frequent until 1649, when the Five Nations smashed Huron complacency by virtually destroying them.

The few Huron survivors fled to the Erie for protection, who, confident of their own strength, refused to hand the refugees over. They had under-estimated Five Nations determination, and in a major battle that followed in 1654, a force of 1,800 Five Nations warriors defeated 4,000 Erie. Although the Erie reassembled and continued minor skirmishing, they too suffered the same fate as the Huron just two years later.

The Five Nations, weak from war and epidemic, then came under attack from the Susquehanna, who defeated the Cayuga and Seneca. A few years later, however, the Susquehanna suffered an epidemic and were easily beaten by the Five Nations. Susquehanna refugees fled and converted to Christianity, after which they became known as the

OPPOSITE RIGHT
Pipe tomahawks, which incorporated a combined metal axe-head and pipe-bowl, were regular trade items and often presented as gifts to favoured Indian leaders. In general, only the axe-head and pipe-bowl were given, and these were then fastened to a shaft of Native manufacture.

BELOW
The Huron tribes, under pressure from the Iroquois League of Five Nations, lost their distinctive tribal identity at a relatively early date and few items of Huron manufacture remain in public collections. This cap, one of only three that still exist, is a rare example of Huron decorative work.

The Eastern Woodlands

Conestoga but were all massacred in 1676 by a mob of Maryland and Virginia Colonists.

The Iroquois and the Algonquin, in addition to their own disputes, were also involved in the hostilities between the French and English, who used traditional tribal rivalries as a means of procuring their own ends. Much of the Huron aggression towards the Five Nations was instigated by the French, since the Five Nations, although declaring neutrality, were obviously unofficially aiding the English, and many of the early Huron victories were clearly determined by the fact that the French gave valuable military assistance.

The period was not, however, without its amusing anecdotes. In 1744 at the Treaty of Lancaster, a spokesman for the Six Nations (the Tuscarora had been given nominal membership in the League in 1715) replied to the English offer to educate Iroquois youths:

> *We know you highly esteem the kind of Learning taught in these Colleges, and the maintenance of our young Men, while with you, would be very expensive to you. We are convinced, therefore, that you mean to do us Good by your Proposal; and we thank you heartily. But you who are so wise must know that different Nations have different Conceptions of things; and you will not take it amiss, if our Ideas of this kind of Education happens not to be the same with yours. We have had some experience of it; but when [our young men] came back to us, they were poor Runners, ignorant of every Means of living in the Woods, unable to bear either Cold or Hunger, knew neither how to build a Cabin, take a Deer, or kill an Enemy, spoke our language imperfectly, were neither fit for Hunters, Warriors, nor Counsellors. We are not the less obliged for your kind Offer, tho' we decline it; and to show our grateful Sense of it, if the Gentlemen of Virginia shall send us a Dozen of their Sons, we will take great care of their Education, instruct them in all we know, and make Men of them.*

(Canassatego, Six Nations Spokesman, Treaty of Lancaster, 4 July 1744)

At the close of the French and Indian War in 1759, the English, now that the usefulness of the tribes was over, left them more or less to their own devices and showed little gratitude or appreciation of the assistance they had received. No attempts were made to prevent settlers squatting on the tribes' best hunting and farming lands, they

were defrauded, and, at times, even kidnapped and sold into slavery. The French, for their part, simply abandoned their former allies to whatever treatment the English cared to mete out to them.

Later, during the American Revolution, large armies containing considerable numbers of Indian allies were used by both the British and the Americans, and some notable Indian chiefs and war leaders were actually given status as commissioned officers; but, again, with the close of hostilities, Indian participation was not rewarded and taking unfair advantage of them continued, leading eventually to a number of Indian uprisings. Again in the War of 1812 between Britain and the United States, Indian allies were used extensively. Tecumseh, who was killed during this latter war, spoke of the rapid decimation of the Algonquin:

> *Where today are the Pequot? Where are the Narragansett, the Mohican, the Pokanoket, and many other once powerful tribes of our people? They have vanished before the avarice and the oppression of the White Man, as snow before a summer sun. Will we let ourselves be destroyed in our turn without a struggle, give up our homes, our country bequeathed to us by the Great Spirit, the graves of our dead and everything that is dear and sacred to us? I know you will cry with me, 'Never! Never!'*

(Tecumseh, Shawnee chief and war leader)

A final Algonquin tribe that deserves separate mention is the Ojibwa-Chippewa, not because their history of large-scale rivalries and involvement in European-inspired wars is much different from the rest of the area – although it may have been less – but because they lived in the north on both sides of the current United States-Canada border, where corn-growing was impossible (their subsistence food was wild rice) and whose lands were not, therefore, subject to white settlement. Today, they are the largest North American tribe (although the Navaho outnumber them in the United States).

The scale of Ojibwa-Chippewa warfare is evident from the fact that it was they who drove the powerful Sioux tribes out of the Woodlands areas and onto the Great Plains, and together with the Ottawa and Potawatomi formed a strong northern confederacy known as the Three Fires. Sharing in the general cultural ethos of the region, the Three Fires developed a shamanic cult known as the Midewiwin, or Grand Medicine Lodge, which reflects Woodland ideas of the magical forces represented in their land.

then slapped his other hand over it. The eagle hesitated, stopped its circling and began to spiral down to earth where it landed dead at Yellow Legs' feet. 'Now get your feathers,' the old man said. Later, when the eagle's heart was opened, the iron spearhead was discovered to be embedded in it.

The importance of the Midewiwin, however, was to initiate young men into the spiritual beliefs of the tribes by 'shooting' them with *migis*, white mussel shells, which were imbued with potent supernatural power. Once shot, the initiate fell dead (entranced) during which he dreamed of all the spirit forces and powers of the Woodlands and became empowered by them. Greater power was acquired through successive initiations, a total of four leading to the status that Yellow Legs enjoyed.

During the Midewiwin, which is also sometimes called the Mystic Society of Animals, the spirits appeared, at least at first, in their animal forms; reflecting the Woodlands dependency on the animal and bird life around them and their close relationship to these. It was said that:

The Indian believes he is a cannibal – all of his life he must eat his brothers and his sisters and deer, and the fish which is the brother. All our lives we must eat off them and be a cannibal, but when we die then we can give back all that we have taken, and our body goes to feed the worms that feed the birds. And it feeds the roots of the trees and the grass so the deer can eat it and the birds can nest in the tree. And we can give back.

An important feature of the Midewiwin was the performance of magical tricks, through which the powers by which an individual was possessed could be demonstrated. Uzauaskogat, or Yellow Legs, one of the Mide priests, was famed for his ability to walk on water, although when observed his power failed him. He did, nevertheless, demonstrate another remarkable ability one day when a crowd of young men, loitering near his lodge, spotted an eagle circling above.

By incessantly complaining that the eagle was too high for them to shoot, in order to obtain its feathers, the young men irritated Yellow Legs to the point where he could bear it no longer. He removed an iron spearhead from his medicine bundle, placed it in the palm of his hand,

Natchez, the Five Civilized Tribes and the Florida Tribes

The Southeastern region of the Woodlands, comprising the Mississippi Delta, Louisiana, Mississippi, Arkansas, Alabama, Georgia, Tennessee, the Carolinas, and Florida, is a region of hot summers and mild winters. Florida, in fact, is almost tropical. In early times, discovered from archaeological excavations, much of this area was occupied by tribes with strict hierarchies who had developed complex temple-mound sites that functioned as ritual centres for large, scattered, urban populations.

Their economy was, like that of most of the rest of the region, based on farming, hunting, and fishing, with corn being a staple crop (although they also grew millet, sunflowers, pumpkins, melons, and tobacco) and, like the other groups, warfare was waged through the amassing of large 'armies' that attempted to occupy neighbouring territories as their own populations expanded. Unlike other Woodlands tribes, however, much of the Southeast was governed by autocratic chiefs who obtained their positions through inheritance, and who, at times, showed a despotic disregard for others.

Natchez

The autocratic nature of chiefs is known from study of the Natchez, who, at the time of Spanish incursions into their area in 1539, still followed the old temple-mound culture of the earlier Mississippians. The Natchez were ruled by a hereditary leader known as the Great Sun, who was both chief and head priest and whose powers were so great that he could, at will, order the execution of anyone who for whatever reason displeased him.

Natchez social life depended on the status one acquired at birth (which depended on the mother's rank rather than the father's) and people were born as Suns, Little Suns, Nobles, Honoured People, and Stinkards or Commoners. They also kept slaves, captured women and children from neighbouring groups (men were tortured and killed) but these had no status unless they were formally adopted into the tribe. Curiously, the Great and Little Suns were forced by custom to marry Stinkards and only the children of female Suns could aspire to leadership. The descendants of male Suns, by contrast, could never rise above the status of Noble.

When the Spanish first came into contact with the Natchez they were surprised at the aggression with which the Natchez defended their lands. The Spanish commander, De Soto, having heard from other Indians that the Natchez were aggressive, tried to deceive the Great Sun of the Natchez, Quigualtam, by pretending to be the younger brother of the astronomical sun from whom the Great Sun claimed descent and whose personification on earth he was thought to be.

Quigualtam, also informed by others who had been closely watching De Soto's movements and monitoring his relationships with other groups, but who had received conflicting reports, decided to impose a test. If De Soto really was the younger brother of the sun then he could no doubt prove this by drying up the Mississippi River. De Soto of course failed, and was driven out of Natchez territory with considerable loss of life to his companions.

Following De Soto's failed attempts to establish Spanish dominion in the area, the Natchez lived relatively unmolested despite their continued conflicts with other tribes – until the early 18th century – when the French established themselves in the Natchez district. Relations with the French were friendly at first, and the Natchez permitted them to establish Fort Rosalie in 1716 on the site of the present Natchez City in Mississippi.

The appointment of a new commandant to Fort Rosalie, who demanded the site of the principal Natchez village so that he might establish a plantation, caused a revolt during which the commandant was beaten to death with a stick by a Stinkard since none of the Natchez warriors would defile themselves by touching him. The French, by bribing tribes hostile to the Natchez and through the defection of the Choctaw, who had promised the Natchez support and then reneged on their agreement, destroyed Natchez culture totally. In the bitter fighting that ensued, the Natchez were scattered and dispersed. Many of their warriors were killed and over 400 from an original total of about 1,000 were sold into slavery in the West Indies. A population estimated at 4,000 in 1715 had been reduced to a mere 50 refugees among the Creek in 1799, by which time the Natchez had lost any sense of a tribal identity.

The Five Civilized Tribes

The Creek, Cherokee, Chickasaw, Choctaw, and Seminole are collectively known as the Five Civilized Tribes, and have a unique cord of attempting to accommodate the demands of the white settlers who moved into their areas. They were friendly to these strangers, and it was largely through their help that the Natchez were defeated. They assumed many European traits; traditional clothing was replaced by cloth, European animals were introduced, and intermarriages were frequent. Many of their chiefs were of mixed Indian-White blood and, despite a few disagreements, the Five Civilized Tribes can be said to have readily adapted to European ideals and to have taken them aboard quite wholeheartedly.

Even so, the transition from a farming, hunting, and fishing economy was not an easy passage. Old Tassel, a Cherokee chief, commented in July 1777 on the demands made upon them by the whites:

Much has been said of the want of what you term civilization among the Indians. Many proposals have been made to us to adopt your laws, your religion, your manners, and your customs. We do not see the propriety of such a reformation. We should be better pleased with beholding the good effects of these doctrines in your own practices than with hearing you talk about them. You say, 'Why do not the Indians till the ground and live as we do?' May we not equally ask, 'Why do not the white people hunt and live as we do?'

Yet despite these reservations, the Five Civilized Tribes introduced the European model of individually-owned farms and livestock, and even rendered their language into a syllabary so that they could print newspapers. In many respects they were more successful than the European occupiers of their territories, since they knew the land better.

But, regardless of their success and willingness to accept European standards, they were harassed by local white settlers, and although they had built roads, schools, churches, and had adopted an administration based on the system of the United States (which, in turn, was based on the constitution of the Iroquois League of Five Nations), they were still persecuted. In 1819, the states of Georgia and Alabama banned tribal governments, and made it impossible for an Indian to testify against a white person. Although these state laws were declared illegal, the Federal Government refused to intervene.

Regardless of this opposition, by 1825 the Cherokee were managing their own affairs, with courts and legal observations based on a

European model, and were producing cotton and wool which were sold on European and American markets. In an attempt to use legal redress to protect themselves, the Cherokee took the state of Georgia to the Supreme Court and won their case; but President Jackson overturned the Court's decision. In 1838-1839 they and other members of the Five Civilized Tribes were forcibly removed from their homelands, some of them in leg irons and manacles, to Indian Territory (now Oklahoma) This 'Trail of Tears' resulted in the deaths of over a quarter of the people who were removed, and is one of the blackest spots in American history.

The Cherokee tribes used numerous lidded split-cane baskets for the storage of small items, such as various vegetable fibres and feathers, that might otherwise have been easily damaged. These items are required for weaving and basket-work as well as being used as decorative attachments for both everyday and ceremonial clothing.

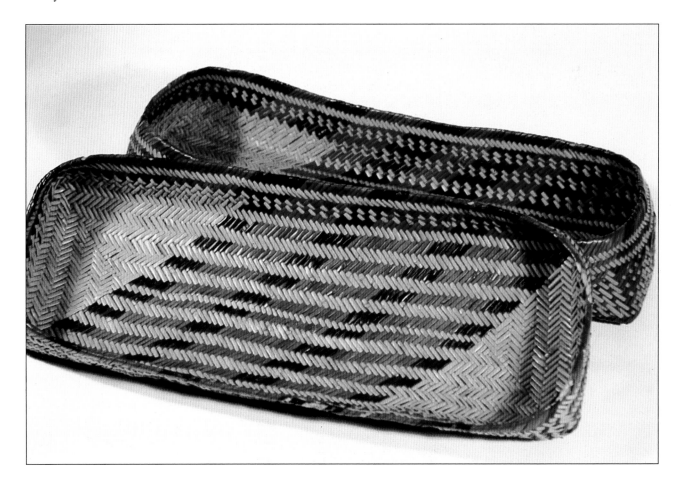

The Eastern Woodlands

The woman shown in this drawing by John White wears the typical scanty dress of Florida tribes from the late 1500s. Note especially the elaborate tattooing that indicates her status as a woman of high rank and nobility.

It appeared as if the Indians could do nothing right. If they opposed the Europeans they were slaughtered by European forces backed up by allies from their traditional enemies; if they acquiesced, they were considered weak and were taken advantage of; and if they adopted European systems and tried to preserve their rights on equal terms these were overturned once they came into the legal system.

A number of Creek Indians successfully resisted these pressures. Alexander McGillivray, the son of a Scots trader and a half-French/Creek mother became the undisputed leader of the Creeks with some 10,000 warriors under his command, and when McGillivray died in 1793 he was one of the wealthiest land- and slave-owners in the Southeast. After McGillivray's death, leadership passed to William McIntosh (whose brother was the Governor of Georgia) who ceded the remaining ten million acres of Creek lands to the United States.

McIntosh's brother campaigned for the removal of Creek Indians to Indian Territory; a treaty of 1825 which guaranteed the Creeks occupation of their lands was annulled by Congressional decree in 1826; fraudulent land claims – which the Creek were not allowed by law to answer – were made by the state of Georgia. Pro- and anti-American factions developed, and McIntosh was executed by his own people for selling off lands to which he had no right.

One section, however, resisted American efforts to dispossess them. Known as the 'Red-Sticks', they began a guerilla campaign against the American forces, and this started a virtual civil war among the Creeks themselves. Pro-American Creeks, together with Americans, and Yuchi and Cherokee Indian allies defeated the Red Sticks and forced them into exile in Florida, where they tripled the Seminole population.

The remaining Creeks, whether pro- or anti-American suffered the same consequence as the other Five Civilized Tribes and were forcibly removed from their lands. The removal of the Creeks began in 1836 when they sadly departed and, forbidden to take property with them, were reduced to destitution. In 1836, Menewa, a Creek chief, looked back on his country as he was marched away in manacles:

> *Last night I saw the sun set for the last time, and its light shine upon the tree tops, and the land, and the water, that I am never to look upon again.*

Speckled Snake, speaking on behalf of the Creek Nation, said:

> *We have heard the talk of our Great Father* [the President of the United States]*; it is very kind. He says he loves his red children. When the first white man came over the wide waters, he was but a little man. Very little. His legs were cramped by sitting long in his big boat, and he begged for a little land. When he came to these shores the Indians gave him land, and kindled fires to make him comfortable. But when the white man had warmed himself at the Indian's fire, and had filled himself with the Indian's hominy, he became very large. He stopped not at the mountain tops, and his foot covered the plains and valleys. His hand grasped the eastern and western seas. Then he became our Great Father. He loved his red children, but he said: 'You must move a little farther, lest by accident I tread on you.' On another occasion he said 'Get a little farther – there is a pleasant country. It shall be yours forever.' Now he says 'The land you live upon is not yours. Go beyond the Mississippi; there is game, there you may remain while the grass grows and the rivers run!' Brothers! I have listened to a great many talks from our Great Father. But they always ended in this – 'Get a little farther; you are too near me.'*
> (Speckled Snake, Creek Chief, 1829)

The Florida Tribes

Typical of the Florida tribes were the Timucua, who came early into conflict with both the French and Spanish and who resisted attempts by them to establish Missions in their area. The tropical swamplands of Florida provided little opportunity for the raising of corn, the mainstay of much of the Woodlands, but did enable the people to obtain masses of fish and wild fruits, which were stored in underground chambers for winter use. They also hunted the crocodile, which was revered both as a food source and as a provider of skins.

Like the Natchez, they had powerful chiefs and a Timucua leader could dictate his wishes. A watchman who had fallen asleep, since the Florida tribes frequently sent out war parties who would try to burn down an enemy village of thatched lodges during the night, might be punished by having his arms broken. Like other Woodlands tribes, those of Florida were capable of sending out armies of many warriors and it was not uncommon for a war party to number in excess of 500 men. Theodore de Bry noted the formation of a war party sent out by Outina whom he described as the 'King' of the Timucua:

Olata Outina, who is considered the king of kings, superior to all others in his number of subjects and his riches, marches with his troops in military formation. He goes alone in the middle of his ranks, painted red. The wings of the army, in the order of march, are composed of young men, the fittest of whom, also painted red, are used as runners and scouts to reconnoitre the enemy troops. Like dogs after wild beasts, they hunt their enemy by scent, and when they find traces of them they run back to their army to report. In the same way that our soldiers pass orders by trumpets and drums, they use heralds who have certain cries for when to halt, or to advance, or to attack or to make some other manoeuvre. They stop at sunset. When they set up camp, they divide into squads of ten, the bravest apart. The king chooses a place in the fields or in the forest to pass the night and after he has eaten and gone to rest the masters of the camp place ten squads of the bravest men in a circle around him. About twenty yards away some twenty other squads form another circle around the first. Twenty yards further away there is another circle of forty and this formation continues enlarging according to the size of the army.

(Theodore de Bry, *Brevis Narratio*, 1562-1565)

Yet despite their fierce independence – Calusa war canoes actually repulsed the first Spanish invasions of the area under Ponce de León – the Florida tribes eventually capitulated. Frequent attacks, aided by Indian allies, undermined their ability to remain aloof from European incursions. The Apalachee, Timucua, and Calusa are now extinct, the remnants of the defeated tribes having been sold into slavery in the West Indies, and only a few Seminole, the last representatives of the once-great Creek Nation, still reside in the Florida Everglades.

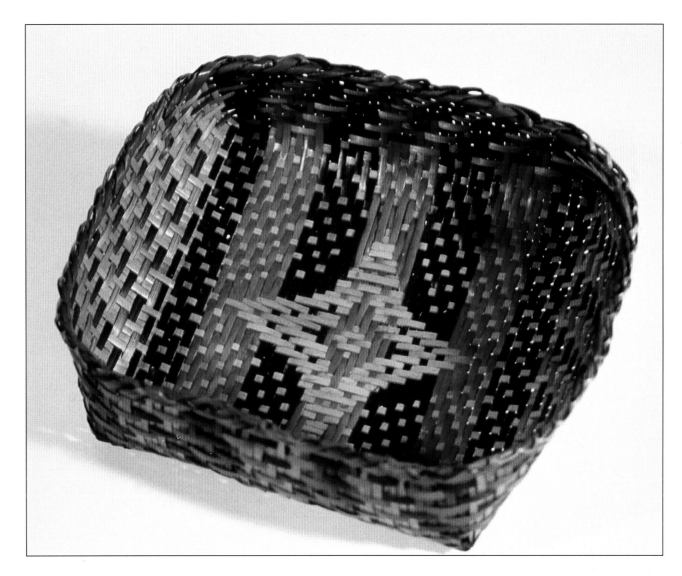

The Cherokee and Chitimacha of the southeastern Woodlands were known for their split-cane baskets decorated with red and black dyes. Such baskets are said to have been used for storing various items to prevent them from 'being wetted by rain'.

Index

Bibliography

The following books are suggested for those who may wish to read more about Native Americans. The listing makes no pretence of being a complete note of works consulted in the preparation of this book. Where a date is listed in parentheses it is the most recent printing known to the author, or is the date of the reprint edition used by the author. This is a list for the general reader, and works of interest primarily to the specialist or only available from specialist libraries have been excluded.

Bancroft Hunt, Norman & Forman, Werner
   PEOPLE OF THE TOTEM: The Indians of the Pacific Northwest, Orbis Publishing, London 1979(1993)

Bancroft Hunt, Norman
   NORTH AMERICAN INDIANS, Brian Trodd Publishing, London, 1991(1996)
   INDIANS OF NORTH AMERICA, Apple Press, London 1992
   WARRIORS, Salamander Books, London, 1995(1996)

Benedict, Ruth Fulton
   PATTERNS OF CULTURE, Houghton Mifflin, Boston, 1924(1989)

Brown, Dee
   BURY MY HEART AT WOUNDED KNEE, Bantam Books, 1972 (but numerous editions)

Buch, Ernest & Forman, Werner
   THE ESKIMO, McDonald Orbis, London, 1988

Catlin, George
   LETTERS AND NOTES ON THE MANNERS, CUSTOMS, AND CONDITIONS OF THE NORTH AMERICAN INDIANS, 1841 (Dover edition 1973)

Coe, Michael; Snow, Dean; Benson, Elizabeth
   ATLAS OF ANCIENT AMERICA, Facts on File, Oxford, 1986

Cremony, John C.
   LIFE AMONG THE APACHES, Roman & Co., San Francisco, 1868(1983)

Drummond, Don E.
   THE ESKIMOS AND ALEUTS, Thames and Hudson, London, 1977(1987)

Ferg, Alan
   WESTERN APACHE MATERIAL CULTURE, University of Arizona, 1988

Hill-Tout, Charles
   THE SALISH PEOPLE, Talonbooks, Vancouver, 1978

Josephy, Alvin M.
   THE AMERICAN HERITAGE BOOK OF INDIANS, American Heritage, 1961

Mooney, James
   CALENDAR HISTORY OF THE KIOWA INDIANS, 17th Annual Report, Bureau of American Ethnology, Washington, 1898(1979)

Neilhardt, John G.
   BLACK ELK SPEAKS, Morrow, New York, 1932

Powell, Father Peter
   SWEET MEDICINE, University of Oklahoma Press, Norman, 1969(1981)

Sturtevant, William C. & Taylor, Colin
   NATIVE AMERICANS, Salamander Books, London, 1991

Walker, James R.
   LAKOTA BELIEF AND RITUAL, University of Nebraska, Lincoln, 1980

West, Ian
   PORTRAITS OF NATIVE AMERICANS, Salamander Books, London, 1995

PHOTOGRAPHIC A

W.E. Channing, Santa Fe, New M
24, 31, 33, 37, 39, 43, 56/57, 76,
National Anthropological Archive
35, 37, 38 (both), 41, 52, 53, 58,
108: Museum of New Mexico, pa
pages 35, 39, 44, 45, 46, 47, 49,
109: Cape Mudge, Vancouver Isl
Museum, British Columbia, page
Columbia, pages 55, 63: Übersee
103: Maximilian, Prince zu Wied
Browning, Montana, page 76: So
page 73: Ian West Indian Museum
68 (both), 69, 78 (both), 79 (both
Collection, London, pages 2, 11,
83, 101: Private Collection, Holla
page 54: Private Collection, Calg